Hot CONFIDENCE WORKBOOK

Conscious Pathways
to Take You from
Mini-Me to *Magnificent*

Nadine Love

Balboa Press books may be ordered through booksellers or by contacting:

Balboa Press
A Division of Hay House
1663 Liberty Drive
Bloomington, IN 47403
www.balboapress.com.au
1-(877) 407-4847

ISBN: 978-1-4525-0643-2 (sc)
ISBN: 978-1-4525-0644-9 (e)

Printed in the United States of America

Balboa Press rev. date: 08/08/2012

This workbook is dedicated to Your positive transformation.

As you honor Yourself
By engaging in your fullest potential,
Your gifts to our treasured earth are beyond measure.

I believe in You and Your true magnificence.

Contents

Introduction
The Invitation

"Twenty years from now you will be more disappointed by the things that you didn't do than by the ones you did do. So throw off the bowlines. Sail away from the safe harbor. Catch the trade winds in your sails. Explore. Dream. Discover."

~ Mark Twain

The fastest and surest way to support you in freeing your magnetic potential and creative outcomes so that you can attract the great relationships you deserve and express your talents and your message boldly and authentically, is to gift you resources to provide the wind under your wings to ensure you fly. That is the reason I created your *Hot Confidence Workbook* and the raft of audios and videos accompanying *Hot Confidence*.

As you discover more of yourself and transform as a result of working through your *Hot Confidence Workbook*, your essential companion to *Hot Confidence*, I know you will literally soar to dizzying heights and surpass the outstanding expectations you have for yourself in this moment. I'm excited for you!

There is inspiration and motivation to be found in the reading of a book. A book falling into your lap at precisely the right moment has the power to transform your life—yet only if you choose to let it. It is what you do with the knowledge, ideas, and concepts you're acquiring that matters. The renowned inventor Charles F. Kettering's words often ring in my ears: "Keep on going and the chances are you will stumble on something, perhaps when you are least expecting it. I have never heard of anyone stumbling on anything sitting down."

You can't fall into Hot Confidence and sizzling self-esteem without taking action to seek it, find it, and cultivate it. In doing so you are ensuring that by putting the system in practice you become competent, and in developing that competence your old fearful feelings that stopped you moving forward, become distant strangers. You'll find, by following the exercises in your *Hot Confidence Workbook*, that you are able to share more of your talents, message, and love with the world each day!

Your journey with your *Hot Confidence Workbook,* as you work through it alongside *Hot Confidence*, will reveal the major reasons that you're not following through on your dreams, visions, and ideas, and help you recognize and master the true magnetic potential within you.

As you apply the practices in these pages and your self-worth grows, you have every chance of becoming the most positive, productive, enthusiastic, decisive, and attractive person you know. Your relationships, opportunities, and finances will thrive as you switch your self-doubt into glowing confidence. It is worth the effort you are about to put in!

Hot Confidence provides you with a roadmap to resilient, rock-solid confidence. Your *Hot Confidence Workbook* gives you the comprehensive, easy-to-follow coaching you need to enable you to access, explore, and appreciate the insights, choices, and opportunities along your route to positive transformation.

The proven, life-changing system in your *Hot Confidence Workbook* incorporates ancient yogic knowledge with cutting-edge findings from Neuro-Linguistic Programming (NLP), positive psychology, and powerful coaching techniques. You'll experience a blend of best practices from East and West, seasoned with over a quarter-century of dedicated experience I have in helping people find their unique voice. If you have the discipline and drive to work through your *Hot Confidence Workbook* thoroughly and apply your self-discoveries, this guide, in conjunction with *Hot Confidence,* will help you become bold in self-expression for passion, wealth-creation, and giving.

If you would like to:

- *Tap into your fullest-potential*
- *Free yourself from self-doubt*
- *Ditch the fear of not getting it right*
- *Raise your self-esteem and self-worth*
- *Let go forever of feeling not good enough*
- *Find alternate ways of dealing with stress*
- *Have the confidence to apply your knowledge*
- *Do something with your life that makes a difference*
- *Find ways to apply your skills, life experiences and abilities*

. . . then apply yourself to the exercises in this handbook, listen actively to the audios, watch the videos, and return to the chapters of *Hot Confidence* often. It is not by chance that you have come across this winning formula. It is a step-by-step, thorough program that will help you transform your life. It's your launch pad to the self-confidence you deserve, attracting the relationships and opportunities you dream of!

On a personal note, all of the exercises, practices, and methods in your *Hot Confidence Workbook* have been thoroughly fine-tuned for you through firsthand knowledge and experience. These are the formulae I apply to my life. They constitute the blueprint of my own transformation from mini-me to magnificent. I have been so frozen by doubt and fear that one time, for example, I lost all sense of direction and did not know where I was or who I was as I stood shivering just a few meters from my home. The one thing I know best in life is how to transform deadening self-doubt into dreams-come-true.

All of my twenty-five years in the personal development and wellness industry—the knowledge gathered; the awards, prizes, and degrees; and the experiences I gained through rebuilding my life from scratch each time in the college of hard knocks—only have value if they can be of service in delivering your fast-track formula to Hot Confidence so that you can live into your magnetic potential and thus create your difference in the world.

Roll up your sleeves and engage with your full attention. The rubber hits the road as you do what it takes to live your transformation. Making your unique difference starts right here! Congratulations. I'm here with you every step of the way.

Reminders as You Set Out

Self-esteem and confidence levels are shaped by past experience, past influences, and our conditioning. The most significant of the three developmental periods described by sociologist Morris Massey is the "imprint period," which is up until age seven.

During these years you were shaped, taking on beliefs, values, and attitudes that steer the course of your life. Your *Hot Confidence Workbook,* along with *Hot Confidence,* will help you make healthy, conscious changes so that you do not continue to chart your course through life based on the impulses, agreements, values, beliefs, and conditioning of a child of seven or less!

It is a law of our universe that **everything is energy**. Your thoughts are energy. Your system is pure energy. The word *system* refers to your physical body as well as the energetic aspects of you that you may not see reflected in the mirror. Eastern traditions call this force field *subtle body,* also known as the *aura*. Self-esteem is an energy frequency, too.

To understand the nature of transformation, it is important to know how our energy systems receive, absorb, and transmit information. Your understanding of your body's subtle energy system will make sense of your blocks and the beliefs that bind you. You will gain new perspectives on how to take your next step toward manifesting your desired outcomes.

Ancient Eastern understanding of how energy is absorbed and rerouted around the body to where it is needed is known as the study of the *chakra system*. *Chakra* is Sanskrit for *wheel* or *disc.* It refers to a spinning sphere of bio-energetic movement flowing from the major nerve ganglia that branch forward from the spinal column. Seven such discs are arranged in a column of energy from the base of the spine to the top of the head. Each of the seven main chakras resonates with a specific principle of human psychological health. They are:

Chakra 1: Known as the *base center* or *muladhara*, also called the *root chakra*—this chakra is concerned with the drive for survival

Chakra 2: Known as the *sacral chakra* or *svadhistana*—the chakra concerned with sexual energy and procreation

Chakra 3: Known as the *solar plexus chakra, manipura, navel chakra, spleen chakra, stomach chakra*, or *liver chakra*—the chakra concerned with power

Chakra 4: Known as the *heart chakra* or *anahata*—the chakra that generates the energy of love

Chakra 5: Known as the *throat chakra* or *vishuddha*—the chakra that governs communication

Chakra 6: Known as the *third eye* or *ajna*, also called the *brow chakra, eye of wisdom*, and *inner-eye chakra*—the chakra that governs intuition

Chakra 7: Known as the *crown chakra, sahasrara*, the *vertex center*, or the *thousand-petalled lotus*—the chakra that governs cognition and spiritual awakening

The chakra system provides the essential energetic framework for gaining insights and awareness into your defenses and specific areas of need.

This *Hot Confidence Workbook* works in conjunction with the first of the two books in the *Hot Confidence* series, structured in chapters that follow the chakra system. The first volume, *Hot Confidence*, builds your strong foundation, taking you from your illuminating first chakra to the lustrous jewel of your authentic, powerful self in your third chakra.

Your journey from mini-me to magnificent continues with the second book in the series, *Heart and Soul of Confidence*. You'll start with a celebration of your right to be unique, spontaneous, and powerful. Your adventure will advance along the rainbow bridge through your heart all the way to your crown center (the seventh chakra), where you'll discover how to fully engage your increased awareness and wisdom. *Heart and Soul of Confidence Workbook* accompanies the second book in the *Hot Confidence* series, providing you with metaphysical mentorship to enable you to attract the relationships, opportunities, and quality of life that is your sacred destiny and birthright.

By virtue of your commitment to increase your confidence and self-esteem, your divine assignment is already being fulfilled in ways you may never realize. You're on track!

MAKING THE MOST OF YOUR *HOT CONFIDENCE WORKBOOK*

Your *Hot Confidence Workbook* has been designed to work with *Hot Confidence* chapter by chapter. You are welcome to write your notes, insights, and observations directly onto the pages.

At the end of each chapter of *Hot Confidence*, you'll find a section called Pivotal Points. These are practical exercises—action steps—that will help you change how you feel and how you relate to yourself. Doing them is important! The Pivotal Points worksheets are the backbone of this workbook.

As well as Pivotal Points, you'll find supplementary information, resources, and additional processes in this workbook to give you even more value and enable you to explore your choices and get to know yourself even more deeply. This material has been carefully structured and sequenced to enhance your experience and growth.

Change does not come about by chance, and techniques don't touch lives if they remain locked in a book. Making your life magnificent requires your action and commitment.

I strongly encourage you to write down your thoughts, experiences, and feelings in a dedicated journal so you can track your progress from mini-me to magnificent. Purchase a special journal for this purpose, or simply follow the worksheets in this workbook that match the Pivotal Points for each chapter.

Organize yourself so that you do your writing in a quiet place where you won't be interrupted. Set aside time so you won't feel rushed. Have a glass of water nearby and do whatever it takes to get comfortable. Reflection and inspiration occur in quiet moments. Make room so they can find you.

In most cases, work through your *Hot Confidence Workbook* from the first exercise to the last. The worksheet sequence is designed to catalyze a steady, authentic connection with your core self and your magnificent potential. Complete each of the Pivotal Points and exercises before you move on to the next.

Alternatively, you can tap into your intuition and select the resource or worksheet that has the most relevance for you, to top up and tone your self-confidence. You can return to the Pivotal Points, exercises, and suggestions offered in this workbook as often as you like, over and over again.

I urge you to continue to apply the practices you learn in this workbook until they become yours and as automatic as your heartbeat. Your transformation and the difference you'll make to yourself, your loved ones, and your community will bring you meaning, fulfillment, and delight.

As you work the *Hot Confidence* program, you'll learn to manage and master your confidence level and self-esteem. You *can* develop self-confidence. Decide to complete the pages that follow. Give yourself your best effort as you complete these life-changing processes. Choose to step into your true, magnificent self. Welcome the hidden potential that has always been within you.

As you work through the deeply personal, pleasurable, intimate, and sometimes confrontational material, you may feel uncomfortable as memories, challenges, and issues surface. The whole spectrum of feelings you experience is to be respected and appreciated. Grant yourself emotional, mental, and physical space to process the courageous, wonderful changes that are around the corner. You are doing great work! There can be nothing more important than your transformation for good.

Remember that quantum physics proves you will attract more of the energy you are. That's enough reason to clear the aspects that are not moving you toward who you want to be, the relationships you desire, and the experiences you'd like to have more of. The inner work you are embarking on is fundamental to shifting your life toward the way you'd love it to be.

Have you reached the moment where all things can be different because you conspire for your own happiness, health, and fulfillment? If you answered "YES!" I'm right beside you as you complete these pages, gifting yourself and the world the radiance that is yours alone, one process at a time. As you move through your *Hot Confidence Workbook,* your light will burn more and more brightly, transforming your mini-me into magnificent you!

Note: It is wise when undertaking personal exploration work of any nature to identify a support person you can trust with whom to share your insights and discoveries. You may wish to enlist the services of a professional mentor, coach, therapist, counselor, or healer as you take this journey. A professional can assist you in managing any emotional, mental, physical, or spiritual issues that may surface for you. In continuing with this Hot Confidence Workbook, *you are accepting full responsibility for your health, well-being, and results.*

1
THE LOST PROPERTY BOX

*You are extraordinary at your core. Choose to **be** that!*

~ Nadine Love, Hot Confidence

Welcome! Here you are. You have reached a turning point. Now is your time.

> "What will *you* ask yourself at the end of your days? Will you be wishing that you had been different in your life? Will you be sad or mad with yourself for having missed out on the things that you know you were capable of? Could you have engaged life more fully? Will you be filled with remorse that you did not give and receive love as boldly as you might have? Are there words you never wrote, sang, or spoke? Could you have mattered more? What will you have done to ensure that your life really stood for something and made a difference?" *~Hot Confidence: Conscious Pathways to Take You from Mini-Me to Magnificent*, Page 2.

THESE ARE MY INTENTIONS AS I TRANSFORM FROM MINI-ME TO MAGNIFICENT:

Fill these pages with your intentions for yourself on all levels. Move out in your imagination to a time when you have already achieved and even surpassed healthy levels of self-confidence and self-esteem. There is no right, no wrong, and nothing to prove as you write freely what comes to you. Let yourself flow with whatever occurs to you.

1. As you become your Hot Confident self, what do you see?

2. As you become your Hot Confident self, what do you hear?

3. As you become your Hot Confident self, what do you feel?

4. As you become your Hot Confident self, what do you tell yourself?

5. As you become your Hot Confident self, what do you notice about your relationships?

THESE ARE MY INTENTIONS AS I TRANSFORM FROM MINI-ME TO MAGNIFICENT:

6. As you become your Hot Confident self, what do you notice about your life?

7. What is it that you intend to accomplish for yourself by completing your *Hot Confidence* program?

8. What else?

9. What else?

10. What have you always (perhaps secretly) wanted to do, be, or have?

Your Purpose and the Lost Property Box

Building your confidence means taking action. It is in the *doing* that great reference points are developed. They become the core of your self-belief. It is said that self-confidence is the memory of success.

Let's start with a setup exercise—setting up your space. For maximum results, I recommend you do this setup exercise as a prelude to every exercise or set of exercises in this book.

Setting Up Your Space

1. Give yourself twenty to thirty minutes so you can take your time with this process.
2. Grab a pen. Use the Finding Your Purpose Worksheet on Pages 6 to 16 to write down your insights and discoveries.
3. Make sure you are in a space that will be uninterrupted.
4. Turn off your cell phone and shut down your computer.
5. Make sure you are warm enough and that you have some water to sip.
6. You might like to open the window for some fresh air.
7. It's optimum if your space is clean and uncluttered. If you wish, clear the space in whatever way you like: you can clap, sound Tibetan bells or a singing bowl, smudge with sage, burn incense or oils, or simply set an intention to cleanse and clear the space in which you sit.
8. Include "sacred" objects near you, such as crystals, flowers, or a special book or painting you enjoy.
9. You can light a candle with intention. This means that as you light your candle you think of something specific. For example: "This candle I light to bring in my creativity" or "I light this candle for my magnificence" or "I light this candle in thanks for my unfolding potential."
10. Settle yourself in your space and take a few deep breaths.
11. Notice the inward and outward flow of your own breath, in your own natural rhythm.
12. Notice your points of contact with the ground, the floor, or your chair.
13. Ask yourself: "Is there anything I need to leave outside my space in order to have an outstanding experience?" Any thought, worry, doubt, or fear that does not support your growth and highest purpose, send away from you as you breathe out.
14. As you breathe in, draw to you all the support, love, and acceptance abundantly available to you.
15. If you wish, welcome your guides, guardians, teachers, mentors, and angels, whether known or unknown, to you in this moment.
16. Take a moment to offer gratitude for this time and for your magnificence. You are perfect as you are.

Note: Do as much or as little of this setup as you deem appropriate. The inner state of respect for yourself and creating a connection with the Divine and your higher self (the wise part of you) are what matters. There may come a time when you carry the sacred space within you so strongly that the external setup is for pleasure more than necessity.

Now you are ready to begin the exercise that the setup exercise just prepared you for. You can download your free audio of the Finding Your Purpose process at www.hotconfidence.com/your_purpose/audio for your ease and quick, comfortable access. Read through the exercise first, to familiarize yourself with the process, then do the exercise while listening to the audiotaped version.

FINDING YOUR PURPOSE *(EXERCISE)*

You have a way inside of you, on an unconscious level, of storing time and of knowing the difference between the past and the future. It's not so much the past that we are interested in right now. It is your future that we are going to focus on.

Please imagine what I am going to suggest. Identify where your past lies in spatial relation to you right now. Is your past beside you to the left or right? Is it above you, behind you, or below you? What I am asking you to do is to get in touch with your timeline. Your timeline is how *you* represent time.

Now I'd like to ask your unconscious mind to create a representation of your future. In which direction does your future lie? Is it above you, in front of you, to the left side, or off to the right side of you? In your mind's eye, note where your future lies.

In your imagination, face in the direction of your future. That's where you're heading, after all. In your mind, take yourself to a time way out in your future. The future is something people look forward to. In your mind's eye, take yourself right out to stand on the far edge of your future and peer into the golden light that extends way beyond anything that you could have ever conceived of as your future.

Allow yourself to be there fully in your thoughts. This is the future space where you are living your dreams and so much more.

Now write down:

1. Who are you?

2. What are you doing?

3. What have you created?

4. What else is significant?

Now turn and look toward the present time. Notice that the golden light of your future is at your back. From this future space, look back to present time. See your journey.

Ask yourself, "How did I get here?"

What special moments held meaning for you?

Identify the key events that brought you from present time to this future place.

Imagine those events. They will make themselves clear to you. You will see those events, and know those events, in your mind's eye. They are the events that lead to the great joy, your successes, and your fulfillment in this future place. Those important events make themselves known to you, now. Allow yourself to be surprised, entranced, delighted, and moved by the events you just experienced—those memorable times that you know you created. Find the moments of the most intense meaning.

Write down a list of these key events.

Select one event.
Ask yourself and write down:

In this significant moment, what am I seeing?

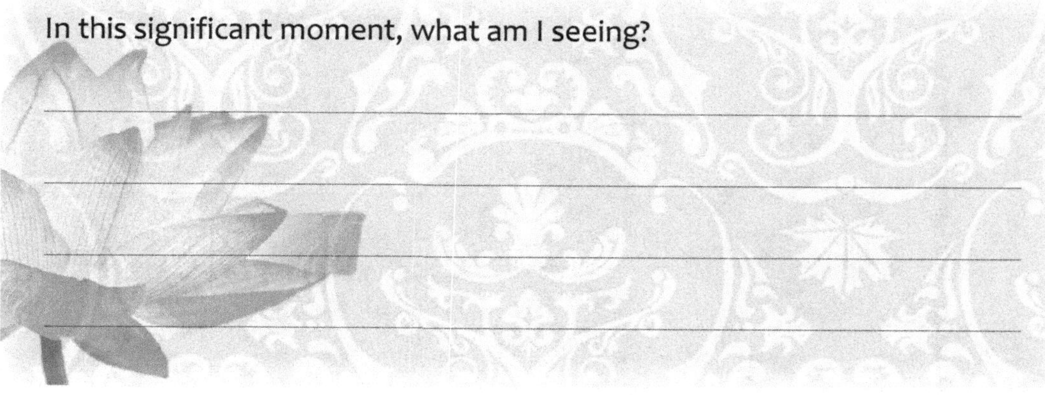

In this significant moment, what am I hearing?

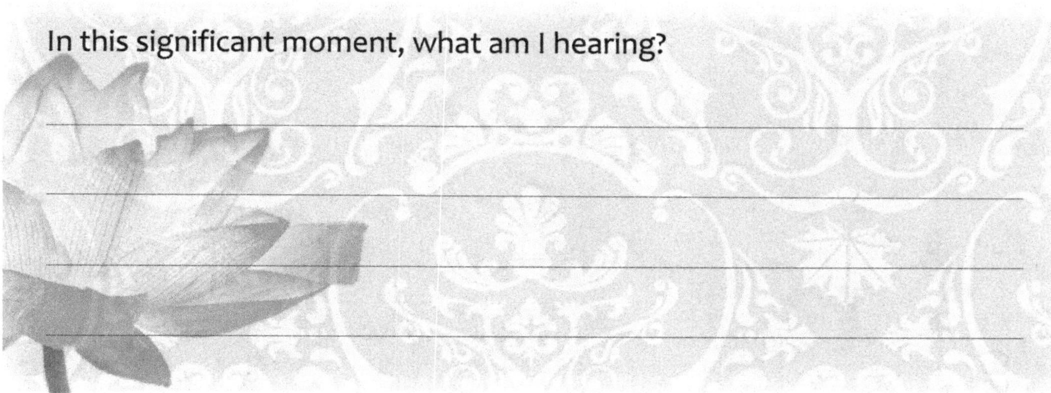

In this significant moment, what am I feeling?

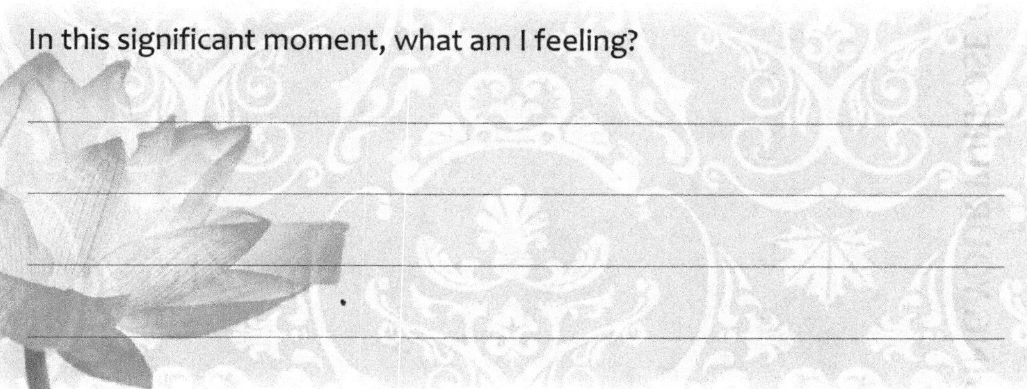

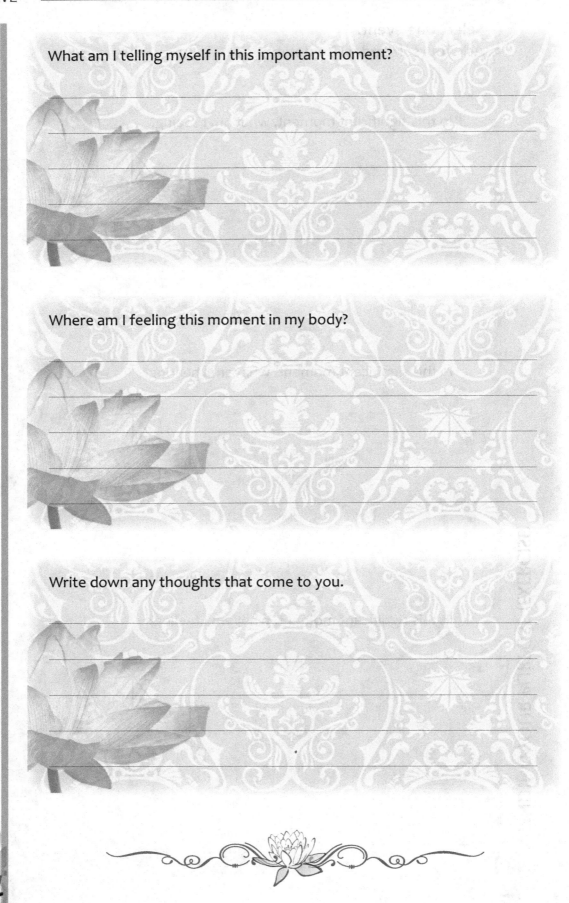

What am I telling myself in this important moment?

Where am I feeling this moment in my body?

Write down any thoughts that come to you.

Capture at least three meaningful moments from the space between your current present and the outer edge of your future. Imagine those times. Let your unconscious mind work for you to construct what those key moments might be.

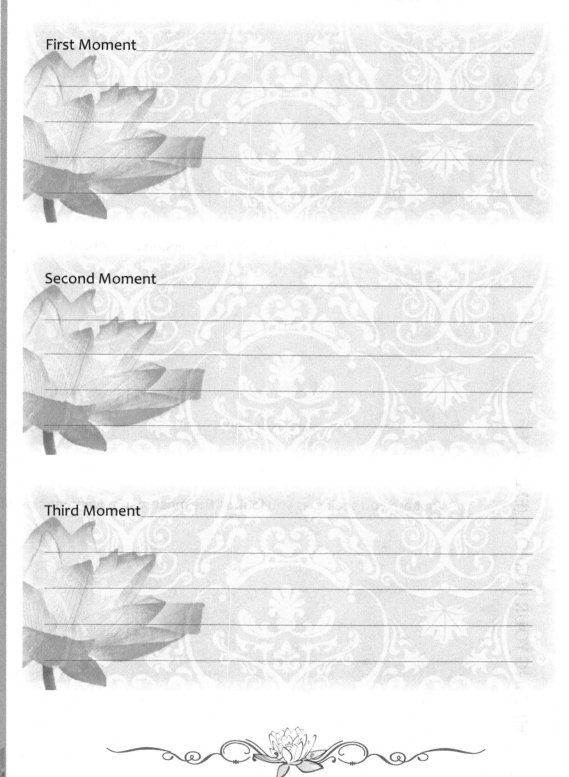

First Moment____

Second Moment____

Third Moment____

Seek out the most poignant, tender, loving times. Capture those. Who are you with? Remember you are looking from the vantage point of your compelling future back on your actual life.

When were you the most outstanding version of yourself?

What are you seeing as you look at the most magnificent version of you?

What are you hearing?

What are you feeling when you are extraordinary?

What sorts of things are you telling yourself, as you are right there in your important moment?

As you are connected with the most magnificent version of you, in your imagination, move to a private, personal space in your own heart and ask yourself:

Where do you have the most sensation in your body right now?

How does your body feel as you connect with the most victorious, successful, and powerful you?

What is my purpose?
What am I here for, on this Earth, to be or to do?

Plant the question like a seed. An answer may come rushing back to you. It may arrive in the form of a thought, an image, a sound, a color, a sentence, a song, or in another form altogether. If the answer does not come to you immediately, that's fine. Your unconscious mind is working on it! Continue with the remainder of the exercise, knowing the answer will be revealed to you soon.

From your lookout point way out at the far edge of your future, notice that somewhere in your past, as you peer back, there is a large box. In this box, there is a random assortment of items, words, images, and objects. As you look more closely, you notice that the box contains all of the ideas, projects, and plans that you had made for yourself and never followed through on. Your box contains all of the words that you wanted to say that were never spoken. Your box houses all of the dreams that never came to fruition. This is your Lost Property Box. All of its contents belong to you.

List the contents of your Lost Property Box. List what you see, what you remember, what you feel. Write without restraint or judgment. Be curious about your list.

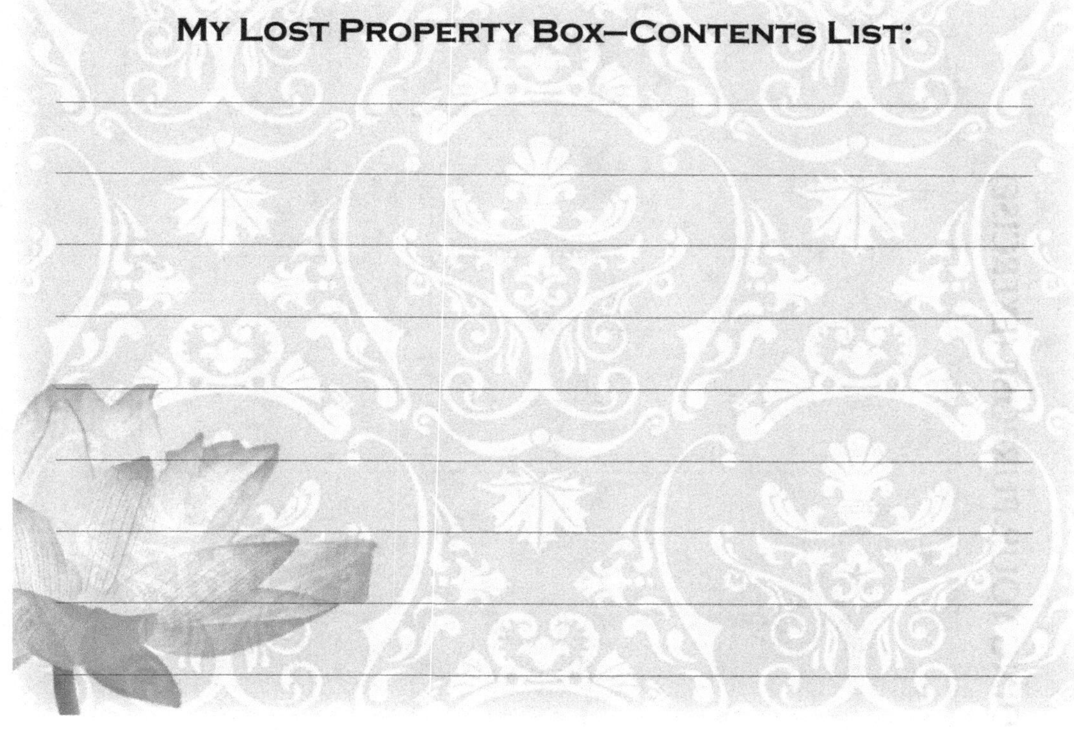

Ask yourself: "If I had high levels of confidence and self-esteem, which of those words or ideas would bounce out of the Lost Property Box and into fruition?"

Have you ever seen a parched, dusty desert burst into flower overnight after a sudden rush of rain? In your imagination, let the life-giving force of desert rain flow through your Lost Property Box. Be open to the flourishing gifts that sprout from this. Is there a project—something that needs to be said or done—just bursting to capture your attention? Who is it you most need to talk to?

Find a special space where you would like to leave your Lost Property Box. It may be in a room in your home, at your altar, in a garden, in a forest, on an island . . . in your imagination, place your box there. Set an intention that any brilliant ideas in waiting will find their way into the box, because this is no longer a Lost Property Box but a Waiting to Manifest Box! The desert rain has made it so.

Turn your attention from the past toward the present. Make whatever connections are needed between the two. Now turn so you can view the entire timeline: your past, your present, and your future. Ask your unconscious mind what future events support the ideas you found in your Lost Property Box and the plans not yet envisioned. Imagine those events taking place in your future.

Now insert those magnificent events into your future timeline, for your greater good and the highest purpose of all. Imagine links between the events of the past and present to the events you just inserted into the future timeline. Go ahead and make those connections now.

Come back now to the present moment. Remember the events you have imagined, and make sure that each one aligns with your purpose in as much detail as you have so far, and make sure each is in harmony with all life. If any are not, revise that now in your mind's eye, so that it is in alignment and harmony.

Whatever connections need to be made on an unconscious plane, your unconscious will make them, bringing together people, events, and circumstances to fulfill the dreams you have just imagined and created from this deep place. Your unconscious will help you accomplish your life's purpose with passion and prosperity, with confidence and self-esteem. Your future timeline is becoming brighter and brighter. Each and every future event and connection supports you all the way back to the now. Are you ready to shine light on the shadows, known or unknown to you, that are stopping you from becoming the most outstanding version of yourself?

Well done. As you breathe, easily and effortlessly, the changes you have already made are continuing to settle into place, bringing to you the vitality, strength, and courage to give yourself permission to be the most brilliant version of yourself right now and into your compelling future. You are wonderful!

TALLYING THE COST OF INACTION

What will it cost you if you choose not to take the steps necessary to raise your self-worth and confidence level?

What will be the cost to others?

TALLYING THE COST OF INACTION

What will your children, your loved ones, and your work colleagues and associates continue to experience? What will they lose out on if, in five years' time, you are still in the same place as you are now with your sense of self?

Pivotal Points

What you'll need

1. *An uninterrupted space*
2. *A pen*
3. *Water to sip*
4. *A voice recorder (optional)*

Pivotal Point #1

Objective

To re-engage flow, to build awareness, to clarify, and to create natural momentum.

Activities

1. List five ideas that you have had that you have not followed through on.

    1. __________
    2. __________
    3. __________
    4. __________
    5. __________

2. List five projects or plans that you haven't done that you wanted to.

    1. __________
    2. __________
    3. __________
    4. __________
    5. __________

3. List three things that you wanted to say to another person but didn't.

    1. __________
    2. __________
    3. __________

Pivotal Point #2

Objective

To build up sensory representations, creating a canvas of pure potential where change can happen in an instant.

Activities

Your unconscious mind loves to work with symbols, archetypes, and metaphors. These are some of the quickest and most entertaining tools for accessing your unconscious. It is in your unconscious mind that transformation happens at a deep level, because new neural connections, pathways, and networks can be formed easily and effortlessly there.

1. Ask yourself the following questions. Answer in terms of your present state of self-confidence, not in terms of the level of self-confidence you aspire to achieve. We are doing "diagnostic work" in the first part of this exercise.

   a. Imagine that your self-confidence is a person, character, or personality. Who or what would that be?

   ____

   b. If your self-confidence had a color, what color would it be?

   ____

   c. When you think about your self-confidence, what are you hearing?

   ____

   d. What do you tell yourself when you think about your self-confidence?

   ____

   f. Where are you feeling your self-confidence most in your body?

   ____

PIVOTAL POINTS

2. Imagine that your life is exactly the way you want it to be, as if someone waved a magic wand over it and suddenly it was perfect.

   a. What are you seeing now when you think of your self-confidence?

   ____

   b. What color is it?

   ____

   c. What are you hearing?

   ____

   d. What are you feeling?

   ____

   e. Where are you feeling that feeling in your body?

   ____

   f. What are you telling yourself when you feel Hot Confidence?

   ____

3. If there were three stepping-stones to get you from your present level of self-confidence to your desired level of self-confidence, what would they be? There are no right or wrong answers: imagine what those steps would be.

   a.______________________________

   b.______________________________

   c.______________________________

4. What is one small step you can take to move from your present level to your desired level of self-confidence?

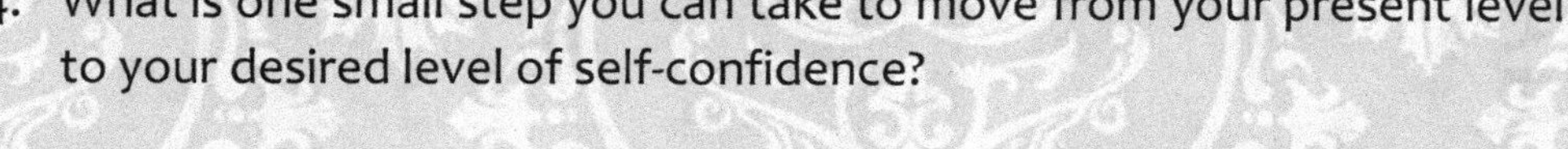

PIVOTAL POINTS

PIVOTAL POINTS

Pivotal Point #3

Objective

To build a healthy connection between yourself and your Source, to improve the quality of your self-communication, and to train your mind to develop a healthy, productive style of self-talk.

Activities

Repeat the following affirmations three times each at least three times a day to embed these concepts in your life:

I open my heart; I welcome the fire of renewal and choose to re-enter life.
I walk forward on my path with confidence and ease.
I now stand proud and tall. I look my world in the eye and smile.
I love and accept myself unconditionally.
I am open to receiving the gifts and blessings of the universe.

2
Believe Hot

"If I have the belief that I can do it, I shall surely acquire the capacity to do it even if I do not have it in the beginning."

~ Mahatma Gandhi

It is no secret that people who exude certainty, confidence, and a firm sense of direction attract easy attention. They are the winners, the leaders, and the people we find irresistible. We want to be around them. Self-belief is attractive and magnetic.

In *Hot Confidence* and your *Hot Confidence Workbook* you have you access to the range of essential elements you need to develop a firm belief in yourself, so that you can cultivate *your* charisma. As you complete these exercises and processes, you'll build your authentic belief that you are *hot*!

Your Mini-Me

Our starting point is to identify the part inside you that is stopping you from being the magnificent person you deserve to be. I call this part your *mini-me*. We'll also determine the flip side of the coin—the ultimate motivator, the inspired you, the brilliant part of you that is ready to triumph.

The part of you that is keeping you small and tripping you up (your mini-me) is in your life because at one time *that part served an important purpose*. In your past, this aspect of you developed in response to a set of circumstances, and it constructed a way of taking care of you. Your mini-me fostered ways to keep you safe and protect you. It found winning formulas to ensure your very survival. For more details and a discussion of self-sabotage, return to this section in your *Hot Confidence* book.

WHO IS *YOUR* MINI-ME? *(EXERCISE)*

What you'll need

1. *An uninterrupted space for ten minutes*
2. *A pen and/or colored pencils or pastels*
3. *A playful, curious, open mind*

Objective

To identify the nature of your self-saboteur for deeper understanding, and to bring on positive change in your relationship with that part of yourself.

Activities

Maintain the non-judgmental perspective of a curious observer. Hear the self-talk; don't get lost in it. Ask yourself these questions, and use your pen or colored pencils to respond:

1. If the part of you that is mini-me was a caricature, person, symbol, or figure, then:

   a. What would it look like?

   ____

   b. What color would it be?

   ____

   c. What would it be wearing?

   ____

   d. What age would it be?

   ____

   e. What sound would it make?

   ____

f. What would its theme song be?

g. If it had words attached, or a personal motto, what would that be?

h. If your mini-me had a general feeling, what would that be?

i. Where do you feel your mini-me most intensely in your body?

j. If your mini-me had a scent or odor, what would that be?

k. If it had a taste, what would that be?

l. What would its landscape or environment look like?

m. What is your mini-me's name? (Make one up.)

2. What would the message be from your mini-me to yourself right now? Write it down.

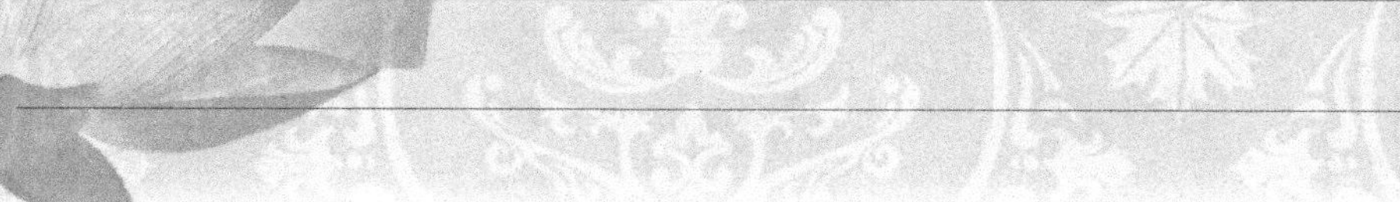

3. How would you respond, from your higher self? Write it down. (Your response must emerge from the wise part of you, not the personality level.)

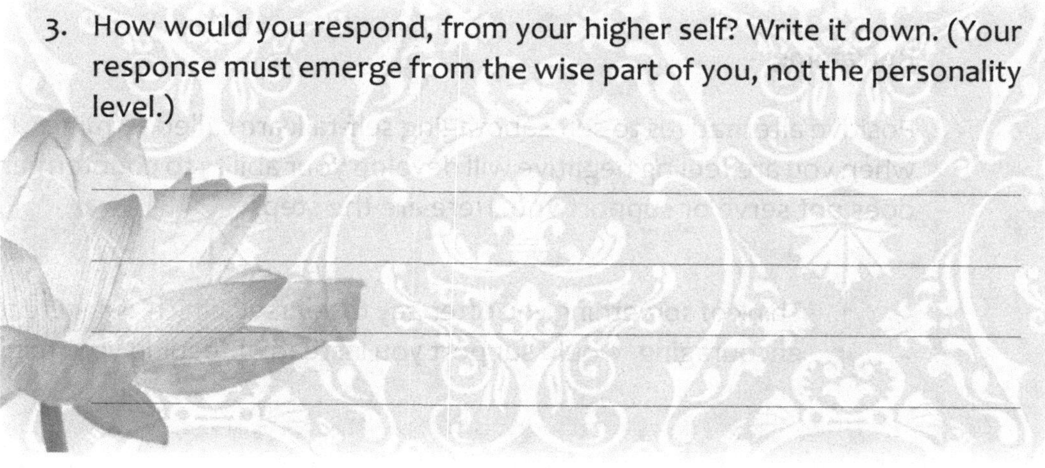

After performing this exercise, you now have a clearer sense of who or what you are dealing with. Well done!

Think through your day so far, and get really specific:

How active was the mini-me you identified for yourself? Rate yourself on a scale of 1 to 10, where 1 is "my mini-me didn't bother me" and 10 is "I procrastinated, didn't do anything I intended to, sat on the couch, ate potato chips, and watched soap operas all day."

(You may not find something major. Any activity counts, even the slightest self-putdown. Was there a thought or action that blocked an opportunity for you that may have had a great outcome? Did you engage in any behavior, self-talk, or thought that kept you small? Did you stop yourself from speaking out or speaking up or standing up for your truths and your core beliefs?)

☐1 ☐2 ☐3 ☐4 ☐5 ☐6 ☐7 ☐8 ☐9 ☐10

SELF-TALK—REFRAMING *(EXERCISE)*

Reframing

Positive alternatives to self-sabotaging self-talk are called *reframes*. Doing a reframe when you are feeling negative will develop your ability to countermand self-talk that does not serve or support you. Here are the steps:

1. Think of something you often say to yourself which, if it were to be more encouraging, would support you instead of feeding your mini-me.

2. In your mind's eye or in a notebook, draw a speech bubble like those you see in comic strips. Write down exactly what you said to yourself.

3. Give yourself five minutes to think about the origins of that thought.

4. Come up with two different positive statements you could say to yourself instead. (For recurring negative self-talk messages, it's best if you write these down to use again next time you hear the same putdown.) Write those sentences here:

   a.____

   b.____

5. Repeat one or both of those reframed sentences three times to yourself.

6. Write down what you noticed or learned by doing this exercise.

7. Apply this technique to your life today and every day. Keep practicing.

What is an Archetype?

Give yourself ten minutes.

1. If you were to take on the persona (archetype) of a rock star for one day and live your life for a whole day as if you were a rock star, how would that change your choices, your thinking, the way you move, and the way you conduct your relationships for that day? As you take this on, allow yourself to experience feelings, physiology, and interactions in completely new ways. What new things do you imagine you would learn about yourself and what are you capable of? Write down at least three new awarenesses:

   a.____

   b.____

   c.____

2. Choose a scenario from your experience in which you engaged with conflict, in whatever way you did.

   a. Imagine, right now, that you are the Dalai Lama, Mahatma Gandhi, or Nelson Mandela. In that same conflict situation, how would you behave if you were that person?

   ____

   ____

   b. How would you behave in the same situation if you were Adolph Hitler?

   ____

   ____

   c. How would you behave if you were your three-year-old self?

   ____

   ____

d. How would you behave if you were your seven-year-old self?

____

____

e. How would you behave if you were the most resourceful, fun, wise version of you?

____

____

f. What did you discover about yourself as you compared being one persona to another? Write down at least three findings here:

i.____

____

____

____

ii.____

____

____

____

iii.____

____

____

____

SAFE HARBOR *(EXERCISE)*

What you'll need

1. *An uninterrupted space*
2. *Water to sip*

Objective

To access clarity, calm, focus, and inner peace, moving to a resourceful state of mind from which the number of choices you perceive as available to you increases.

Activities

Use this exercise any time you

(a) feel unsafe or confused,
(b) find yourself making self-sabotaging choices that keep you small and limit your opportunities, or
(c) need to find respect and compassion for the part of you that keeps you down (the mini-me).

1. In your mind's eye, imagine that you step into a blue bubble. In the bubble there is an image—an image of a safe harbor, a calm and contained bay for you to sail into and take refuge in. This is a place where you have your own space entirely.

2. Into your safe harbor, imagine bringing:

    - Your favorite colors
    - Sounds that you love (music or sounds of nature)
    - Your favorite foods and fragrances
    - The feelings of the successes you've had in your life
    - The energies of people you hold dear
    - The supportive energies of people who love you unconditionally

3. In your thoughts, move into your safe harbor with all of those strong resources in place there. From this safe, abundant, full place, observe with respect your original wounds, and acknowledge the positives in your life as it is.

Everything you need is within you, now. This is one of my favorite Anthony Robbins incantations and a principle of NLP. Take this on as absolutely true. Believe that you have all of the resources right inside you at this very moment to be the hot, confident you that you aspire to be!

Where Are You?

It's time to check in with yourself and evaluate where you are in terms of your levels of confidence and self-esteem. In the Reality Check Exercise, you'll get an up-close look at what comprises your self-esteem and confidence, where your strengths are, and where you might like to focus for improvement.

For an example of the Reality Check Exercise, return to *Hot Confidence* and discover how Sally, a photographer in her early thirties, was surprised to learn she had more self-esteem than confidence. Sally discovered the specific areas she needed to focus on to change how she felt about herself so that she could attract more clients and her ideal partner.

Sally summed up her findings: "I was able to see clearly, from taking the Reality Check, that I needed to develop my self-confidence in order to become more flexible. I noticed how hard it is for me to bounce back after I've taken a knock in life and also how difficult it is for me to say how I feel or what I want. Mostly I don't even know what I want. It's hard to ask for help. It was invaluable to see that emerge so clearly. Now I know it's related to a lack of confidence in myself. I was also able to acknowledge, from doing the exercise, how I am good at looking after myself physically and at organizing my finances. I feel better about myself already, for knowing that."

It's time for you to score yourself. When you take your evaluation, bear the following three points in mind:

1. A point on one scale is sometimes closely related to a point on the other scale. It is useful to compare scores between the two scales in such cases.

2. You may like to define for yourself a range of desired functioning rather than just one number, to give yourself the flexibility to meet a variety of situations. (After three months, Sally took the Reality Check again, and reflected: "I'm constantly at a range in both my self–esteem and confidence between 7 and 10. I live around an 8 or 9 on both, in all areas. Now I know where to modify my choices. It's fabulous!")

3. You can compare where you are now on the scale with where you would like to be at a given point in time. Record both numbers, and in a few weeks retake the test to see if your "now" score comes closer to your "target" score.

REALITY CHECK *(EXERCISE)*

What you'll need

1. *An uninterrupted space*
2. *A pen*
3. *Water to sip*

Objective

To measure your levels of confidence and self-esteem.

Activities

In your mind, enter a personal, private space where there is no right or wrong and nothing to prove. This is a compassionate space, a judgment-free zone that supports your growth, wisdom, health, and happiness. Create this now. Ask your unconscious mind to be fully present.

Read through the following two charts, scoring yourself on each item on a scale of 1 to 10 (1 meaning "rock bottom: almost none," 10 meaning "outstanding: peak state"). Ask yourself for a number between 1 and 10 in terms of

(a) your current level of confidence or self-esteem, and

(b) your target level (where you'd like to be one month from now)

Get curious about your results, and write them in your journal or workbook with today's date alongside your results. You will be able to refer to these measurements to track your progress as you move through the *Hot Confidence* book and workbook.

	Confidence	My Current Rating (Scale of 1 to 10)	My Target Rating (Scale of 1 to 10)
1.	I am adaptable and flexible in all situations, most of the time.		
2.	I am easily able to bounce back from challenges in reasonable time.		
3.	I am willing to take calculated risks. I feel the fear and do it anyway.		
4.	I am willing to have a go at new experiences and to embrace fresh opportunities.		
5.	I have secure trust in my skills and abilities.		
6.	I am able to be autonomous and self-directed in life.		
7.	I am able to take charge, appear in control, and be competent in handling challenging situations.		
8.	I am able to accept and embrace criticism constructively.		
9.	I am able to speak up and say what I feel, believe, and stand for without fear.		
10.	I am able to make decisions and accept responsibility for the consequences.		
11.	I have a firm trust and faith in myself.		
	My Confidence Total Score:		

	Self-Esteem	My Current Rating (Scale of 1 to 10)	My Target Rating (Scale of 1 to 10)
1.	I am clear about what I will or won't do for others, maintaining clear boundaries.		
2.	I manage and value my time.		
3.	I have an ability to say "no" or "yes," holding true to my capabilities and values.		
4.	I take care of myself well on all levels: emotional, physical, spiritual, and intellectual.		
5.	I manage my finances responsibly, taking care of my money within the ecology of my life.		
6.	I am able to define and direct myself toward the outcomes I desire.		
7.	I accept full responsibility for my feelings.		
8.	I am able to experience joy.		
9.	I am able to appraise myself realistically and accept both my shortcomings and my skills and competencies.		
10.	I have a positive self-regard independent of my appearance, wealth, status, or relationships.		
11.	I am free of any dependencies and addictions.		
	My Self-Esteem Total Score:		

Reality Check: Self-Rating Score Sheet

We each have an optimal range of functioning. This differs slightly from person to person. A total somewhere between 80 and 100 out of a possible 110 on in the rating charts above would give you consistent results and the capacity to live life to the fullest, whatever that means for you.

Date:________________________________

My Confidence Total Score:________________________________

My Self-Esteem Total Score:________________________________

Compare your results and notice where your higher score lies. Do you have more confidence than self-esteem, or vice-versa?

My Key Realizations:

This is what I found most interesting:

____

These are the key areas I must focus on for confidence building:

____

These are the key areas I must focus on for self-esteem building:

____

These are the first actions I will take, within the next twenty-four hours, to raise my confidence, based on what I learned here:

____

These are the first actions I will take, within the next twenty-four hours, to raise my self-esteem, based on what I learned here:

____

This is the date I will review my progress:

____

This is the date I will retake the Reality Check:

____

If your current scores are below 65 (out of a possible 110 for each scale), then your reservoirs are low, and you could be enjoying your life a whole lot more. You could be more effective and more in command of your destiny—with some serious tweaking applied!

Note: Set yourself regular dates to take your Reality Check. You can do this once per quarter (on the 1st of January, 1st of April, 1st of July, and 1st of October); once per month, on the new or full moon; or on special days such as your birthday or the anniversary of an event.

Establish the dates that work for you and stay consistent so that you can track your progress, identify where you need to focus, and celebrate your growing confidence and self-esteem. Mark your calendar, now.

When you have retaken the Reality Check to rate your self-esteem and confidence again, using these two same charts, compare your previous scores with your current ones. Write your answers here or in your journal.

Date: ______________________________

My Confidence Total Score: ______________________________

My Self-Esteem Total Score: ______________________________

Compare your results and notice where your higher score lies. Do you have more confidence than self-esteem, or vice-versa?

My Key Realizations:

This is what I found most interesting:

____

These are the key areas I must focus on for confidence building:

____

These are the key areas I must focus on for self-esteem building:

____

These are the first actions I will take, within the next twenty-four hours, to raise my confidence, based on what I learned here:

____

These are the first actions I will take, within the next twenty-four hours, to raise my self-esteem, based on what I learned here:

____

This is the date I will review my progress:

____

This is the date I will retake the Reality Check:

____

How well are you moving toward your goal scores?

____

On which points are you progressing more slowly?

____

What more can you do to increase your confidence and self-esteem?

____

Over the course of this quest for Hot Confidence, if you apply the tools, you will experience the joy of living life from the place of your greatest potential. May you enjoy the discoveries that await you in this chapter's Pivotal Points.

PIVOTAL POINTS

What you'll need

1. *An uninterrupted space*
2. *An open mind and a commitment to your own transformation*
3. *Water to sip*

PIVOTAL POINT #1

Objective

To gather evidence of your competencies and capabilities, to build positive reference points, and to increase positive self-awareness.

Activities

1. Create your Credibility Inventory. Allow plenty of time—thirty minutes to an hour. Compile a list of your achievements including everything that you have experience in. For example, you could list that you are a mother, father, sister, brother, daughter, son, loyal friend, and so forth. Or that you have travelled, emigrated, written a book, won an award, or completed a college degree. Maybe you know how to drive a car or play a musical instrument, or you excel at a sport. These are your credibility factors. List all you can think of.

2. Add three credibility factors to your list each day for a week.

3. Copy your Credibility Inventory and keep it somewhere you can see it. Refer to it when you need to remind yourself of your experience, value, and worth.

My Credibility Inventory

List your achievements including everything you have experience in.

Pivotal Point #2

Objective

To increase your awareness of how well you care for yourself.

Activities

1. Intentionally do one thing each day for the next seven days in each of the following life areas, taking care of:

    a. Your body
    b. Your mind
    c. Your spirit
    d. Your education or learning
    e. A relationship that matters to you

2. List nine ideas in each of the five categories, now.

    a) Ideas to take care of my body

    ____
    ____
    ____
    ____
    ____
    ____

    b) Ideas to take care of my mind

    ____
    ____
    ____
    ____
    ____
    ____

c) Ideas to take care of my spirit

____

____

____

____

____

____

d) Ideas to take care of my education and learning

____

____

____

____

____

e) Ideas to take care of a relationship or relationships that matter to me

____

____

____

____

____

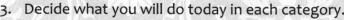

3. Decide what you will do today in each category.
4. Take action on at least one of the five in the next ten minutes and another within the next hour.
5. At the end of each day, write in your journal any insights you have had as a result of your conscious choice to take care of yourself.

PIVOTAL POINTS

PIVOTAL POINTS

PIVOTAL POINT #3

Objective

To increase awareness of your innate wisdom.

Activities

1. Go to www.hotconfidence.com/energytools/internal_pendulum, and access your free audio download.

2. Listen to the Internal Pendulum audio.

3. Day 1 (today!): Decide that for the next hour you will listen to your internal pendulum and follow your inner guidance.

4. Day 2: Decide that for the whole morning you will listen to your internal pendulum and follow your inner guidance.

5. Day 3: Decide that for the morning and the afternoon you will listen to your internal pendulum and follow your inner guidance.

6. Day 4: Decide that for the morning, afternoon, and evening you will listen to your internal pendulum and follow your inner guidance. Select your hour of focus for day 5.

7. Of the affirmations you've been repeating from the last chapter, continue your regimen with the ones you find most potent and useful, and discontinue any that don't resonate with you. Keep a list in your journal or in this *Hot Confidence Workbook* of affirmations you are currently using and another list of affirmations you found effective but have stopped and may wish at some time to come back to. You will find journal pages for My Daily Affirmations (for the affirmations you are presently repeating) and My All-time Favorite Affirmations (for the affirmations you know you'll return to) at the end of this workbook. Keep your My Daily Affirmations list up to date to keep your confidence creating current!

8. Repeat three of the following affirmations three times each, at least three times a day, to embed these concepts in your life. (Of the affirmations you've been repeating from the last chapter, continue your regimen with the ones you find most potent and useful, and

discontinue any that don't resonate with you. Update your Daily Affirmations and All-time Favorite Affirmations lists at the end of this workbook.)

I follow my inner drumbeat with joy and commitment.
I appreciate the magnificent possibilities within me.
I focus on the positive actions that feed my body, mind, and soul.
Centered and powerful, I embrace my life as an exciting adventure.
I believe in me.

PIVOTAL POINTS

3 PURPOSE, PRESENCE, AND VALUES

"The purpose of life is a life of purpose."

~ Robert Byrne

This section in your *Hot Confidence Workbook* gives you the practical steps to take to put your personal mission into your own words, align with yourself, and be present to your higher calling. Your dedicated efforts in this chapter will be rewarded by setting in place your foundation for resolute self-esteem and self-confidence.

Reminder:

The difference between a goal and a mission is that a mission hs an intense sense of purpose behind it. Your life mission is the greatest mission of all, your divine assignment - what you are on Earth to accomplish. I call this your Personal Umbrella Mission or Heart Stone. Once you are clear about your Personal Umbrella Mission, every choice and decision can be measured against it. This ensures that you maintain integrity between who you are and how you express yourself in the world. Your private and professional decisions align to create a reality that is fulfilled, prosperous and peaceful.

Your core codes are your values. These principles define who you are, and they direct your life, although you may not have conscious awareness of them. Your values have a profound and far-reaching impact on your life. They influence your capability, behaviour and environment. Behaviour is what you do. Values are what you expect of yourself and how you represent yourself.

In this chapter you will discover your Paths to Presence, put Self- Acceptance firmly on your map, clarify your Personal Umbrella Mission, complete Your Personal Change Audit and determine your Core Codes so that you set in place your solid foundation for resolute self-esteem and self-confidence.

You and the Eight Paths to Presence *(Exercise)*

Once you have read through the section in *Hot Confidence* on "Getting Present," you can further integrate your understanding of how to become more present by applying your newfound knowledge to yourself, right now. This exercise is designed to bring you deeper awareness of the areas in which you would benefit from increased awakening. You'll discover where you need to engage even more to improve the quality of your life, your attention, and your results.

On a scale of 1 to 10, where 1 is "very little" and 10 is "fully and completely," rate yourself right now on each of the Eight Paths to Presence:

1. Being present to yourself		
2. Being present to your basic needs		
3. Being present to your purpose		
4. Being present to your choices		
5. Being present to your outcomes		
6. Being present to your message		
7. Being present to your respondent		
8. Being present to the moment		

Think of a situation in your life in which you would like to be fully present. Rate yourself as you expect yourself to be in the situation. Now make some adjustments mentally, noticing which paths of presence require attention. Make those changes in your mind.

Rate yourself again.

These were the improvements I noted:

____

____

____

ACCEPTING SELF

Self-acceptance is a private contract with yourself to be at peace with who you are in the now. It is one of the most sacred agreements you can choose to have, providing a baseline for your interaction with others and for your experience of the world.

Below is a list of beliefs that challenge self-acceptance. Even if the words aren't exactly the same as the ones you would pick to express how you feel, do you hold any of these or similar beliefs?

• There are certain ways I should be.	
• Suffer to be successful.	
• No pain, no gain.	
• Rich or successful people are thieves.	
• If I accept myself the way I am, I won't ever change.	
• If I don't feel guilty, I'll continue doing bad things.	
• Life is hard.	
• Self-acceptance is vain, selfish, and insensitive to others.	
• People have to pay their dues.	
• If I accept the way I am, I'll stop growing.	
• Guilt and feeling bad are necessary to keep people on track and honest.	
• You can't have your cake and eat it too.	
• Optimistic people have their heads in the clouds.	
• If success, happiness, or self-acceptance became my priorities, I'd be inconsiderate of others.	
• I can't change—this is just how I am.	
• The world is unfair and cruel.	

Rate each of these beliefs on a scale of 1 to 10, where 1 is "I hardly believe this" and 10 is "I believe this 100 per cent" Choose the three beliefs that scored highest out of 10 and write them down.

1. ____________________

2. ____________________

3. ____________________

For each of these beliefs you have listed, write down:

a. Where did the belief come from?

Belief One: ______________________________

Belief Two: ______________________________

Belief Three: ______________________________

b. Whose voice you hear in your head when you think of that belief?

Belief One: ______________________________

Belief Two: ______________________________

Belief Three: ______________________________

c. What would a person who held this belief have to believe?

Belief One: ______________________________

Belief Two: ______________________________

Belief Three: ______________________________

d. Evidence that this belief is true

Belief One: ______________________________

Belief Two: ______________________________

Belief Three: ______________________________

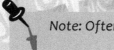

Note: Often you will find there is no evidence at all to back the old belief.

If you want to address the beliefs that are holding you back and causing you pain, apply the Seven Secrets of Self-Acceptance in *Hot Confidence* and notice the difference.

YOUR PERSONAL UMBRELLA MISSION: MY WORD FEST!

Come up with as many words as you can to express your life's purpose.
Write fast without editing any words out.

Your Personal Umbrella Mission

Knowing your Personal Umbrella Mission is very important. Once you are clear on it, every choice and life decision can be measured against it. This ensures that you maintain integrity between who you are and how you express yourself in the world. It means your private and professional decisions line up to shape a reality that is fulfilled, peaceful, and prosperous.

Your Personal Umbrella Mission has an intense sense of purpose behind it. It is the reason you came into this world—what you are on Earth to accomplish. It's "umbrella" because it covers and includes all lesser missions and goals in your life.

Refer to *Hot Confidence* to find out the impact of not knowing or being congruent with your life mission. You may already have experienced this. If you feel you are struggling against the flow of life in terms of health, finances, relationships, and motivation, it is highly likely that the exercise that follows has the potential to herald a significant breakthrough for you.

Objective

To determine your own Personal Umbrella Mission.

Activities

Allow one to two full hours for this exercise. Give yourself permission to accept whatever surfaces. A voice recorder works well, as it allows speaking with your eyes closed in an uninterrupted manner. Alternatively you can close your eyes, contemplate, and then write your answers. If you're using a voice recorder, switch to paper and pen once the brainstorming part of the exercise is over.

1. Set an intention to come up with a sentence that describes your life purpose and reflects who you truly are.

2. Brainstorm words that you feel might have something to do with your life's purpose. Give yourself permission to come up with as many words as you can, fast and without editing any out.

   •
   ____

   ____

3. Group words into categories based on whatever criteria you know to be right for you. You'll notice some words are "banner" words, meaning they are umbrella terms (or global terms) that include the meaning of some of your other words.

4. From all the words you have, circle those that you instinctively feel best reflect something important about your life purpose. Often these are your banner words that contain the heart of who you are.

5. Copy the circled words onto a new piece of paper. Then play with those words, moving them around to finally form a sentence or two that describes your life's purpose. You'll know you have it when you can tell yourself something like: "This is me. This sounds like me. This looks like me. This feels right." This is your Personal Umbrella Mission.

6. Write your Personal Umbrella Mission here, where you can always look at it:

7. Become familiar with your Personal Umbrella Mission. Memorize it.

Well done!

Note: Because you have accomplished your Personal Umbrella Mission here, this exercise is not repeated in the Pivotal Points for Chapter 3 in this workbook. In Hot Confidence, this exercise appears in Pivotal Points at the end of Chapter 3.

YOUR PERSONAL CHANGE AUDIT

How do you fare with change? Here are twelve questions to support you in understanding how you respond to change in your life. This will benefit you in terms of gathering a greater knowledge about yourself so that you are able to move to a state of self-acceptance. In this case, self-knowledge recovers choice and power.

1. The changes I find easiest to handle are . . .

2. The changes I find most challenging are . . .

3. When I see change coming, I . . . (Do you freeze? Do you run toward it? Have you learned to embrace it?)

4. When change catches me by surprise I . . .

5. The change I'm most proud of is . . .

6. The change I wish I could do over again is . . .

7. Strengths I overuse in times of stress or change include . . . (For example, I have a tendency to go into overdrive or hyperactivity mode. I ride a total adrenaline rush, power through, and often I crash at the end. This predisposition is a good thing to be able to harness and focus. There are times when it is very useful to go like a dynamo. However, when used to an extreme the result is unhealthy.)

8. Abilities I underuse in times of stressful change include . . . (For example, abilities I underuse include the ability to look at the big picture. I also neglect my ability to go into a state of heightened awareness. I may not be as tolerant or compassionate as I strive to be. I may not exercise my ability to step into someone else's moccasins and see the world from their perspective. I may override my ability to move into swift meditation. I underuse my humor and ability to go to laughter to diffuse a situation. All of these abilities would be extremely useful in times of change.)

9. What I dislike about the way I handle change is . . .

10. What I can acknowledge myself for about the way I handle change is . . .

11. Ways others can help me through this current transition are . . .

12. Who is on my team?

Congratulations for having already discovered how to become more present. You've found out more about your relationship with change and identified your life mission. In the Pivotal Points section of this chapter you will continue to lay your firm foundation for building your resilient self-confidence and self-esteem as you construct your success and triumphs list, learn two simple meditation techniques to help you become more present, and explore your core values. Strengthen yourself by practicing the suggested affirmations at the close of this chapter.

PIVOTAL POINTS

PIVOTAL POINTS

What you'll need

1. *An uninterrupted space*
2. *A pen and your journal*
3. *A voice recorder (optional)*
4. *Water to sip*

PIVOTAL POINT #1

Objective

To turn remembered successes into reference points that support your budding confidence and self-esteem.

Activities

1. List your successes and triumphs, as far back as you can remember.

2. Give each success and triumph a title.

3. For each success and triumph, list the primary emotion you felt.

4. In your journal, for each success and triumph, describe what happened in fewer than five sentences. (Here you are identifying the story about what happened.)

5. In your journal, for each success and triumph, write down what you learned or the growth you gained from the experience.

6. What does this set of remembered successes and triumphs tell you about yourself?

7. Will remembering these successes and triumphs give you strength and optimism when you face other challenges in the future? If so, keep this list on hand and consult it whenever you start to doubt yourself.

PIVOTAL POINTS

PIVOTAL POINT #2

Objective

To learn two meditation techniques that focus the mind, cultivating the experience of presence.

Activities

Here are two meditation techniques you can practice that will focus your mind and develop your ability to be present to the moment. The first is an eyes-open meditation; the second is done with eyes closed. For meditation to be most effective, it should be practiced for about twenty minutes at least once a day (twice a day ideally).

1. This exercise can be done outdoors or indoors. Sit up straight, yet settle yourself comfortably. It's okay to have back support. Set the intention of sitting still for about twenty minutes. (Make sure phones and other distractions have been turned off and that you won't be interrupted.) You will want to know when twenty minutes is up, so place a clock nearby where you won't have to shift to see it (no fishing for your watch or cell phone). Do not set an alarm, as this would be deeply jarring.

   Choose a point of focus—some tiny spot in the room on which to center your vision. It might be the tip of the leaf of a plant, the corner of a knick-knack across the room, even a spot on the wall. The point of focus you select should be straight in front of you, so your head or eyes won't have to turn left or right to see it. It should be a little below eye level, so you are looking down slightly when you gaze at it.

   Sitting upright, allow your gaze to settle on your chosen point of focus. Just look at it, with no expectations. When you become aware of sounds or thoughts, don't worry about them. Just let your attention favor the point of focus, gently returning to it when you notice your mind has wandered. It's very important to be accepting when you notice sounds and thoughts; resistance—even in the form of slight annoyance—destroys the mind's ability to settle.

   Keep your eyes on your point of focus. It will get blurry or fuzzy as you become relaxed, and your eyes may start to close. Keep your eyes open and looking at the object, but allow your vision to blur when it wants to. In other words, don't try to hold the object of focus clear in your vision—it's *supposed* to get fuzzy. This state of expanded perception is sometimes called "soft focus."

Try not to move for the entire twenty minutes. When you think the time may be up, it's okay to look at the clock. You'll find after practicing this a few times that your body remembers what twenty minutes feels like, and you'll naturally come out of the meditation without needing to check the time. When you are finished, you can move around, but wait for a couple of minutes before getting up. This will allow your mind to transition without jarring it from the state of deep stillness back to activity.

2. The eyes-closed meditation is a variation of the eyes-open meditation. Start with the eyes-open meditation (in the exercise above), and when you feel at home practicing that, try it with your eyes closed. The procedure is the same except for the following differences:

    - The point of focus is your awareness itself rather than an external object.

    - Begin by closing your eyes and taking a few slow, deep breaths, just observing your breathing. Do this until you feel settled and comfortable.

    - Allow your attention to shift from your breathing to the space behind your thoughts. Let your awareness observe itself.

    - There *will be* thoughts. At times you may even get lost in thoughts and forget you are meditating. You may even doze. Don't resent any of this. It's all natural. When you become aware you've been nodding off or absorbed in thoughts, simply return your attention to the space behind the thoughts—the simplest state of awareness that the thoughts arise out of.

    - This meditation feels blissful but a little odd at first, because it reverses the direction of your attention from its customary outward direction to inward. You may feel like you are looking backwards inside your own head, or sitting inside your head, or your head may feel tingly or expanded. The more you allow your attention to simply focus back on itself, the more blissful and still you will become. You are experiencing your true nature—the consciousness that is the heart of your being.

PIVOTAL POINT #3

Objective

To identify your personal values and your career or business values.

Activities

1. Write down seven statements that begin with "I feel my best when . . These are statements you know to be true about yourself at those times when you are most self-congruent. It may help to think about a time when you felt truly motivated in your personal life or at work. Here are a few examples of the many things you might write (remember there are no wrong answers; your answers will reflect your uniqueness): "I feel my best when I apply myself fully," "I feel my best when I'm honest," "I feel my best when I speak up in intimidating situations," or "I feel my best when I confront my fear."

   a.______________________________

   b.______________________________

   c.______________________________

   d.______________________________

   e.______________________________

   f.______________________________

   g.______________________________

2. Write the answers to each of the following questions in a free-flowing way. Write down the first words that come into your mind, accepting every quality that comes up. Keep writing your answer until you have nothing more to write. Then move to the next question. When finished, look over your list and circle words that appear more than once. Order your values in terms of your most significant value to the least significant. Come up with your top five values. An alternate way to do this exercise is to record your answers to each question on a voice recorder so you can talk in a fluid way, and then play back your responses and create your lists. To identify your personal values, answer the following questions: (You may need extra paper for this exercise)

PIVOTAL POINTS

a. How do you spend your time?

b. What do you think about?

c. At a time when you were truly happy, what had to be present?

d. How do you fill your space?

e. How do you spend your energy?

f. In what areas of your life are you the most organized?

g. What triggers a big reaction in you?

h. For what purpose do you do what you do?

i. In what areas of your life are you the most focused, disciplined, and reliable?

j. In your mind's eye, what do you see right now?

k. What do you talk to yourself about?

l. What do you talk to other people about?

m. In which situations do you feel most comfortable?

n. What causes do you support?

o. What goals do you have?

p. What are your dreams for your future?

q. What factors are the most important to you in your situation?

r. What is important to the other significant people in your life?

s. What do you believe to be right?

t. What do you believe to be wrong?

u. What has to be true for you to get what you want?

v. In what circumstances do you say *must*, *should*, *must not*, or *should not*?

3. When you have completed your list, ask yourself, "Are these values helpful to me in my life? What values might help me to get better results?"

4. You may like to consciously add in a value you notice is missing and take it on. To help yourself do this, think of a person who has achieved results in the area in which you would like to improve. Ask yourself, "What would this person value if they were in my shoes?" You can then come up with the name of a value that expresses what you need to work on.

5. Write your top five personal values on a small piece of paper and keep it in your wallet. Read it again and again until you know your values by heart.

6. Repeat all the steps above, only this time with a focus on your career or business values. In creating this particular value list, make sure that in the top two items you have a financial or money value present. (Words you might choose include *financial freedom, wealth, prosperity, profit,* and so on.) When focusing on your business values, ask yourself:

   a. At a time in my career when I was truly motivated, what needed to be present?

   b. If all of the above were present, what would cause me to intentionally leave my career or job?

7. Choose three of the following affirmations and repeat three times each, at least three times a day, to embed these concepts in your life. (Of the affirmations you've been repeating from previous chapters, continue your regimen with the ones you find most potent and useful, and discontinue any that don't resonate with you. Update your Daily Affirmations and All-time Favorite Affirmations lists at the end of this workbook.)

I accept myself fully and completely.
I deeply and completely love and accept myself.
I am loving and accepting of others and myself;
I create lasting friendships.
I accept all things the way they are.
I deserve the very best in life.
I am at peace with myself.
I accept and appreciate the reality I have created.
I am fully and completely at peace with myself.
I choose love and acceptance.
I accept and release everything in my life
that is beyond my power to change.
I receive the gifts and surprises of the universe
gladly and gratefully now.

PIVOTAL POINTS

4
Make the Dragon Your Pet

"The cave you fear to enter holds the treasure you seek."

~ Joseph Campbell

The first step to freedom from fear is to identify and acknowledge which fears are stopping you; it's impossible to change something you don't recognize.

Your fears were created by your ego to keep you small. At one time they may have protected you by sounding alarms when appropriate. Your ego feels threatened when you grow and expand, and creates panic and breakdowns to cause you to remain in familiar, known territory. This is so even if that space is unhelpful for you and does not serve achieving your dreams.

The level to which you are willing to be open and engage your beliefs and fears determines the quality of lasting and resilient confidence you forge for yourself. The more you give of yourself to this section in *Hot Confidence* and in completing the exercises in this workbook, the greater will be your transformation.

YOUR "FREEDOM-FROM-FEAR INVENTORY"

Objective

To reprogram your subconscious mind to free yourself from fear.

1. Circle the fears below that you relate to as yours, including those that you don't want to admit to!
2. Eradicate them, one by one, so they no longer affect you, by:
   a. Determining where the fear came from and how you got it
   b. Looking for proof in the form of evidence that the fear is true
   c. Raising the possibility that the fear is false
   d. Challenging the fear
   e. Objectively telling yourself you can be, do, or have anything: "I can be, do, or have anything I choose."
   f. Asking your self, "How would my life transform if I chose not to have this fear anymore?"

Fear of not being loved	Fear of not being good enough
Fear of not belonging	Fear of being abandoned
Fear of being unfulfilled	Fear of being alone
Fear of being rejected	Fear of failure
Fear of being overwhelmed	Fear of the unknown
Fear of asking for money	Fear of poverty
Fear of success	Fear of what others will think of you
Fear of making mistakes	Fear of being wrong
Fear of your own power	Fear of being vulnerable
Fear of humiliation	Fear of becoming greedy
Fear of having what you want	Fear of not being able to pay the bills
Fear of not doing things right	Fear of being different
Fear of not fitting in	Fear of being hurt emotionally

Fear of feast and famine	Fear of being found out
Fear of being fully authentic	Fear of facing your deepest truth
Fear of not having clients	Fear of not getting it
Fear of losing	Fear of not remembering
Fear of not having enough	Fear of not measuring up
Fear of not fully grasping concepts	Fear of not finishing
Fear of losing freedom	Fear of confrontation
Fear of speaking up	Fear of growing too big
Fear of losing it all	Fear of being exposed
Fear of what others will think if you make money	Fear of not filling a list or a class to capacity
Fear of being insignificant	Fear of being significant
Fear of having to get a job	Fear of not getting a job
Fear of not being wealthy	Fear of relying on yourself alone
Fear of letting yourself down	Fear of missing out on life

Other things you can do to take the quantum leap toward being more *you* and less steered by the fears that hold you from your fullest potential are:

1. The best way to get over a fear is to face it—walk right into it. Walking into fear is ***never*** as challenging as you think it will be.

2. Affirmations (You can refer to the end of each chapter of *Hot Confidence* and this workbook for suggestions for proven and resourceful affirmations.)

3. Visualizations

4. Tapping or Emotional Freedom Technique (EFT)

5. Meditation and guided meditations

6. Neuro-Linguistic Programming and hypnosis

7. Surround yourself with people who are demonstrating qualities and successes you would welcome into your own life.

8. Set "Freedom from Fears" dates in your calendar ideally twice a month. New moon and full moon are excellent times to clear out self-limiting fears and experience the quantum leaps that result from befriending your fears. It's resourceful to set times to clear fears rather than waiting for a situation in which you are triggered, in order to give yourself the gift of taking care of your relationship with your fears.

> Remember:
>
> Fear is energy, and as such can be changed into another form in an instant.

These are the three things I learned about myself by taking the Freedom from Fear Inventory.

____

____

____

This is what I now know about myself and my relationship with Fear.

____

____

____

____

____

____

RECOGNIZING THE FIVE FOUNDATION-SHAKING FEARS

Take your first leap to freedom from the fears that hold you back by finding your own words to define them. The following exercises will guide you safely through the process. It's time to identify how the Five Foundation-Shaking Fears show up in your life so that you can choose to make changes that will improve your health and increase opportunities and joy.

The **Five Foundation-Shaking Fears** are: (For examples of things you might say to yourself, refer to *Hot Confidence*, Chapter 4.)

1. **The fear of not being loved**
2. **The fear of not belonging**
3. **The fear of not being good enough**
4. **The fear of being abandoned**
5. **The fear of being unfulfilled**

For each of the Five Foundation-Shaking Fears, in the space provided below, write what you say to yourself regularly.

1. **The fear of not being loved**

____

____

____

☐1 ☐2 ☐3 ☐4 ☐5 ☐6 ☐7 ☐8 ☐9 ☐10

2. **The fear of not belonging**

____

____

____

☐1 ☐2 ☐3 ☐4 ☐5 ☐6 ☐7 ☐8 ☐9 ☐10

3. **The fear of not being good enough**

☐1 ☐2 ☐3 ☐4 ☐5 ☐6 ☐7 ☐8 ☐9 ☐10

4. **The fear of being abandoned**

☐1 ☐2 ☐3 ☐4 ☐5 ☐6 ☐7 ☐8 ☐9 ☐10

5. **The fear of being unfulfilled**

☐1 ☐2 ☐3 ☐4 ☐5 ☐6 ☐7 ☐8 ☐9 ☐10

Rank your fears on a scale of 1 to 10 as they relate to your life. 1 means "not relevant at all" and 10 means "this is totally applicable to me."

Notice which of the fears you choose to be affected by most.

1. What would happen if you did not feel this way?

2. How would your life be different?

3. What is the very first step you could take for each of your examples above, to choose to respond differently?

There are also five financial fears that serve to destabilize people. These are:

1. The fear of financial failure and the resulting abandonment and loneliness

☐1 ☐2 ☐3 ☐4 ☐5 ☐6 ☐7 ☐8 ☐9 ☐10

2. The fear of not having enough now or in the future

☐1 ☐2 ☐3 ☐4 ☐5 ☐6 ☐7 ☐8 ☐9 ☐10

3. The fear of putting yourself out there and asking for more money

☐1 ☐2 ☐3 ☐4 ☐5 ☐6 ☐7 ☐8 ☐9 ☐10

4. The fear of seeming greedy if you have money

☐1 ☐2 ☐3 ☐4 ☐5 ☐6 ☐7 ☐8 ☐9 ☐10

5. The fear of financial struggle and going broke

☐1 ☐2 ☐3 ☐4 ☐5 ☐6 ☐7 ☐8 ☐9 ☐10

Rank your financial fears on a scale of 1 to 10 as they relate to your life. 1 means "not relevant at all" and 10 means "totally applicable to me."

You will gain a clear perspective on the areas that require your positive attention in order to create positive transformation.

Layered on top of the five financial fears are ranges of limiting beliefs around achieving wealth. It is little wonder there is so much anxiety in this area. By writing down the beliefs you hold about wealth, you'll be able to identify your sensitive areas and the self-held beliefs that sabotage your financial well-being.

List your beliefs about wealth here:

For your "Freedom-from-Fear Meditation" (an audio recording), go to

www.HotConfidence.com/energytools/freedomfromfear/audio.

TRANSFORMING MASH-ME'S

The powerful process of clearing limited beliefs is designed to guide your positive self-communication. I've coined the term "mash-me" to indicate the thoughts, self-talk, and comments you make about yourself that diminish you and crush your confidence.

Mash-mes include all of the limiting beliefs and fears listed in your "Freedom-from-Fear Inventory" that you completed above and in the "Clearing-Limiting-Beliefs Inventory" that follows. Your "Clearing-Limiting—Beliefs Inventory" will help you to effectively stop yourself when you find yourself engaging in a mash-me, revise your language, and realign with what you'd prefer to think and attract.

The first step to freedom from your limiting beliefs is to identify and acknowledge which beliefs are in your way. It's impossible to change something you don't recognize.

Objective

To reprogram your subconscious mind to free yourself from limiting beliefs.

1. Circle the limiting beliefs in the chart below that you relate to as yours, including those that you don't want to admit to!

2. Eradicate them, one by one, so they no longer affect you, by:

    a. Determining where the belief came from and how you got it
    b. Looking for proof in the form of evidence that the belief is true
    c. Raising the possibility that the belief is false
    d. Challenging the belief
    e. Objectively telling yourself you can be, do, or have anything: "I can be, do, or have anything I choose."
    f. Asking yourself, "How would my life change if I chose not to believe this anymore?"

I'm not enough	I'm not worth it
I don't know enough	I don't deserve it
I'm afraid to shine	They'll laugh at me
Who am I to do this?	I can't have it all

I have nothing to offer	Success is for other people
They might find out I'm a fraud	They won't pay for this
In this economy, no one will hire me	How can I accept money for something I love to do?
I can't compete	I can't accept money for something that's easy for me to do
Now's not the time	My knowledge and expertise is common sense and basic
I don't deserve to succeed	They won't want what I offer
I'm a failure	I have to be fake for them to like me
I get overwhelmed	They won't like me
I can't do this	I'm not good at anything
I'm not good at marketing/selling myself	I don't deserve nice things
I have to struggle to know I'm really working	I have to struggle to know I've earned it
Life is hard	I can't manage a full practice
If I attract clients, I get overwhelmed	If I attract a partner, it always goes wrong
I don't have what it takes	I'm too disorganized
I shouldn't charge for this	I'm not a good speaker
Who am I to do this?	It can't be easy; it must be hard
Who do I think I am, anyway?	I need to learn more
I won't be able to have a life	I don't know enough
A man is supposed to take care of me	I don't have time to market

My target market is too small	People won't/don't want what I provide
I won't have any fun	I don't like to deal with people
People always let me down	There's too much competition/too many competitors
My target audience has no money	My target audience won't pay
I'm not motivated enough	I don't have all the answers
If I promote I'll be like a real estate agent or used car salesman	I never win; why even bother to get in the game?
I don't have money to do that	They'll think I'm greedy
They'll think badly of me	I'll have to do a half-hearted job
I have to discount to have clients	I will take on too much
I will spread myself too thin	I'm too busy already
People won't pay my full fee	People won't pay what I'm worth
I'm not as good as he/she is	I'll never make good money at this
I'll never remember it all	I won't know what to say
People don't listen to me	This won't work for me/my business
I can't afford to get help	My industry is too unstable
It's a cruel world out there	It's a dog eat dog world
It will all be taken away when I get it	This is hard work
I won't be able to have a life	I might have to travel a lot
I might have to give up travelling	It's not appropriate for a woman to be successful
It's not appropriate for a woman to promote	I'm too old

I'm too young	I don't like to sell
I'm not a morning person	I'm already too scattered
I have to work hard and long hours to succeed	If I'm powerful and successful people won't like me
If I am successful people won't like me for myself	I can't possibly charge that much!
My partner will leave me if I'm successful	I can't do it all again
I don't like meeting new people	I am useless at networking
I'm not a lucky person	I'm boring

Other things you can do to help you take the quantum leap toward being more *you* and less steered by the beliefs that hold you from your fullest potential are:

1. Affirmations (You can refer to the end of each chapter of *Hot Confidence* for suggestions for proven and resourceful affirmations.)
2. Visualizations
3. Tapping or Emotional Freedom Technique (EFT)
4. Meditation and guided meditations
5. Neuro-Linguistic Programming and hypnosis
6. Surround yourself with people who are demonstrating qualities and successes you would welcome into your own life.
7. Find a Positive Belief Buddy. Invite a close friend, loved one, or mentor to be your accountability partner with specific regard to clearing the beliefs that do not support you and installing resourceful beliefs that do!
8. Set "Positive Belief" dates in your calendar a minimum of once a month—ideally twice a month. New moon and full moon are excellent times to clear out the belief clutter and install affirmative beliefs.

Taming Your Dragon

This rating chart will help you keep track of the progress you are making in terms of taming your dragon. It is useful to keep conscious tabs on your "fear dragon"—the creature responsible for undermining so many of your hopes, goals, and dreams.

Score yourself on a scale of 1 to 10, where 1 is low and 10 is high, as to how you rate in terms of your fear dragon at each of the following points in time. You can add your own milestones to continue to monitor your increasing self-assurance.

Fear Dragon Rating Chart	Date	Score out of 10
Before I read *Hot Confidence*		
After completing Pivotal Points at the end of Chapter 1		
After completing Pivotal Points at the end of Chapter 2		
After completing Pivotal Points at the end of Chapter 3		
After completing my "Freedom-from-Fear Inventory"		
After completing my "Clearing-Limited-Beliefs Inventory"		
After completing my "Taming Your Dragon" visualization		
After completing Pivotal Points at the end of Chapter 4		
After completing Pivotal Points at the end of Chapter 5		
After completing Pivotal Points at the end of Chapter 6		
After completing Pivotal Points at the end of Chapter 7		

An important reminder: There are only two things you can change: *How you perceive something* and *the procedure by which you do something.*

In Chapter 4 of *Hot Confidence* and in this workbook, you have discovered new perspectives on your fears and applied learned techniques for transforming the ways you have dealt with fear and its impact on your life. Very good!

Pivotal Points

What you'll need

1. *An uninterrupted space*
2. *A pen*
3. *Water to sip*

Pivotal Point #1

Objective

To gain self-knowledge by exploring your mindset regarding five esteem-related factors.

Activities

1. Apply The Mindset Tracker by taking this little test. Score yourself on a scale of 1 to 10 for each of the following, where 1 is "very low attention (almost none)" and 10 is "maximum, high-quality attention":

   a. Looking after your physical and emotional needs
   ☐1 ☐2 ☐3 ☐4 ☐5 ☐6 ☐7 ☐8 ☐9 ☐10

   b. Creating a positive self-image
   ☐1 ☐2 ☐3 ☐4 ☐5 ☐6 ☐7 ☐8 ☐9 ☐10

   c. Fostering good and clear relationships
   ☐1 ☐2 ☐3 ☐4 ☐5 ☐6 ☐7 ☐8 ☐9 ☐10

   d. Developing social confidence
   ☐1 ☐2 ☐3 ☐4 ☐5 ☐6 ☐7 ☐8 ☐9 ☐10

   e. Developing workplace confidence
   ☐1 ☐2 ☐3 ☐4 ☐5 ☐6 ☐7 ☐8 ☐9 ☐10

2. Once you have rated yourself, notice which areas require greater attention from you. Write a Self-Commitment Action Statement for each such area. It should include a sentence explaining what you pledge to do in order to move your score to a nine or ten for that factor. Be specific. ("I will take better care of myself" is a general statement and, as such, is not very useful. By contrast, "I will think twice before saying yes to something I'm asked to do" is a specific commitment that could prove quite helpful if you routinely sabotage yourself by taking on projects you don't want in order not to displease people.)

PIVOTAL POINTS

Your Self-Commitment Action Statement must be about what *you* can do or influence—it must not be dependent on anyone else or their behavior, responses, or actions. This is all about creating a glowing, resilient core of self-respect and self-confidence!

Self-Commitment Action Statements:

1. Looking after your physical and emotional needs

2. Creating a positive self-image

3. Fostering good and clear relationships

4. Developing social confidence

5. Developing workplace confidence

PIVOTAL POINTS

Pivotal Point #2

Objective

Strengthening your positive reference points to develop your inner strength.

Activities

1. Write a list of successes you have had. Your achievements can be big or small. List at least ten things.

2. Write a list of at least ten things for which you are truly grateful.

3. Write a list of at least ten good things you have done.

PIVOTAL POINT #3

Objective

To formulate your own Fear-Buster Plan in accord with your unique needs.

Activities

Let's start with a summary of the Eleven Tools for Taming Your Dragon:

1. Know Yourself and Know Your Fears
2. Respect Your Fears
3. Respect Yourself
4. Befriend Your Dragon
5. Get Up, Get On, and Lean In
6. Exercise
7. Take Action
8. Sing or Whistle
9. Live in the Here and Now
10. Think and Talk Positively
11. Rest and Relax

PIVOTAL POINTS

1. Reread the expanded version of these tools in the corresponding section of this chapter in *Hot Confidence*, or listen to the downloadable audio of the same at www.HotConfidence.com/energytools/tame_your_dragon/audio. Write what you learned or noticed about yourself here.

2. Identify the tools that you can apply most easily in your life right away. Be specific about how you will integrate these strategies in your life. List your answers here:

3. Identify the two tools that you find most challenging. Determine what you will do to take your first non-threatening step toward using each of these two tools to tame your dragon. (Come up with one step for each tool.)

   a.

b. ____

____

____

____

____

4. If you have not yet done so, complete your "Freedom-from-Fear Inventory" (found earlier in this chapter of your *Hot Confidence Workbook*), and choose a specific fear to master over the next week. You can focus on another fear with your plan for the following week, and so on. Remember: change can happen in an instant. Fear is energy, and an imprint of the meaning you have given to something. That's all it is. Each time you act from your heart rather than from fear, you contribute to the evolution of consciousness, to collective human wisdom, and to the healing of Mother Earth. Open your heart to the reality that love is the answer. Your love for yourself is the light that makes all things in your orbit shine and prosper.

5. Repeat the following affirmations three times each at least three times a day to embed these concepts in your life. (Of the affirmations you've been repeating from previous chapters, continue your regimen with the ones you find most potent and useful, and discontinue any that don't resonate with you. Update your Daily Affirmations and All-time Favorite Affirmations lists at the end of this workbook.)

I am loved, I am safe, and I am free to choose.
I accept myself as I am now—always and in <u>all</u> ways.
I perform loving actions that bring me health, happiness, and abundance.
I am a perfect expression of love, and I express my love unconditionally to myself and to all others.
I choose to honor the divinity that I am in all events and in all things, with knowledge, understanding, and compassion.

PIVOTAL POINTS

5
Bring on the Sunlit Bowl

"Our very survival depends on our ability to stay awake, to adjust to new ideas and to face the challenge of change."

~ Martin Luther King Jr.

As you pick up the tempo, your transformation to magnificent is assured if you continue to engage in a deeper exploration of your relationship with survival, home, prosperity, and health. The processes in this chapter set the cornerstones of your foundation for trust, self-nourishment, and Hot Confidence!

In Chapter 5 of *Hot Confidence*, you met with the energy center known as your base chakra. In Sanskrit, this chakra is called *muladhara*, which means *root*. Resilience or weakness in this chakra affects every other subtle-energy center (chakra) above it. Fear is the main emotional state that challenges the first chakra.

You've already made tremendous headway with this state and gained excellent awareness into your fears. You'll recall that unacknowledged fear keeps the base chakra from healthy functioning and blocks you from moving forward. Your appreciation of your fear enables you to face it, track its origins, and transform it. Through this insight and knowledge, greater confidence is yours.

RECLAIMING YOUR RIGHT TO BE HERE

Objective

To develop your awareness around your essential, instinctual sense of your right to exist; to develop confidence and self-esteem, your birthright to exist and to have must be reclaimed.

Activities

Circle the phrases below that are true for you right now.

Note, answer as it is for you and not as you know it "ought to be" for you.

I know I have a *right to do* the following:

- Take up space
- Be heard
- Hold an opinion
- Deserve love
- Establish my individuality
- Take care of myself
- Have whatever is needed to survive
- Be prosperous

I feel I have a *right to have*:

- Time to myself
- Love
- Pleasure
- Money
- Ease
- Freedom
- Success
- Praise
- Fun

Take a look at both of these lists and reflect on what is true for you. Add to these lists as you notice areas in your life in which you feel you do not have a right *to exist* or *to have*. When you have reclaimed your birthright to exist and to have, you'll then manifest the stability, trust, physical health, grounding, and wealth you desire for yourself.

Your Four Confidence Columns

Self-Commitment Action Statements

Build the sturdy structure you need to support your magnificence by attending to the Four Confidence Columns consistently. Start right by shaping your Self-Commitment Action Statements for each of the four columns. Write clearly and boldly exactly what it is that you intend to do, starting in the next twenty-four hours, to improve each column.

1. Relationships

2. Exercise

3. Sleep

4. Touch

Bounce-back-ability Tools

As you progress you will find that even though you are putting time and effort into your transformation, every now and then a life challenge comes your way. If you can see these times as opportunities to measure how far you have come and test out your newfound confidence, esteem, and skills, then even the darkest times can be perceived as your greatest gifts.

To support you through the tougher hours, here are the five strategies I've found most effective in helping me to bounce back. I call them "Bounce-back-ability Tools." I believe this is a fine moment for you to receive them and to plant what I call Your Safety Tree. This refers to an imaginary internal support to keep you grounded, aligned, and connected with your highest purpose and your Personal Umbrella Mission, regardless of life's storms.

1. **Set a bigger intention.** Right now give yourself the gift and the inner lift of writing down an intention for yourself that is larger than the one you had, in the most important area of your life to you.

2. **Clear your limiting beliefs.** Revisit the "Clearing-Limiting-Beliefs Inventory" and apply the tools that work for you.

3. **Surrender to what is.** (This is a big one.) Consciously move yourself into a state of acceptance.

4. **Let go of the past.** Actively stop stories and dramas you are creating. Return to the Eight Paths to Presence techniques to assist you in becoming engaged in the present moment.

5. **Trust in what is to come.** Believe there is a miraculous resolution just around the corner. That's right! There is.

In Pivotal Points you will be encouraged and supported in your quest for inner security, outstanding self-care, and glowing self-trust. As you develop your strong, attractive presence, your ability to ground and center yourself is reinforced through the exercises. You'll experience an affirmed right to be here and delight in the right to have what you need to survive—if you continue to apply yourself fully.

Have fun as you strengthen and maintain your base chakra through applying what you learned in Chapter 5 of *Hot Confidence* and by working through the exercises in the Pivotal Points below.

Pivotal Points

What you'll need

1. *An uninterrupted space*
2. *A pen*
3. *Water to sip*

Pivotal Point #1

Objective

To clear relationships for conscious confidence and to gain inner freedom and awareness by identifying unclear relationships in your life.

Activities

Ask your unconscious mind to be fully present during these exercises, for your good and the good of all.

1. Think of someone you really love. Notice how you feel and where you experience that feeling most in your body. Become aware of the quality of your love. Clear the screen of this image in your mind.

2. Now think of something you feel neutral about. It could be an object, a place, or a time of day. Notice how you feel and where you experience that feeling most in your body. Become aware of the quality of your neutral feeling. Clear the screen in your mind.

3. Next think of something that causes you to have a big, negatively charged reaction. It could be an act of injustice, a behavior you don't like, or a memory that unsettles you, for example. Notice how you feel and where you experience that feeling most in your body. Become aware of the quality of your reaction. Clear the screen in your mind.

4. Think of something else you feel neutral about. It could be an object, a place, or a time of day. Notice how you feel and where you experience that feeling most in your body. Become aware of the quality of your neutral feeling. Clear the screen in your mind.

5. List the names of two or three people, the thought of whom provokes a feeling of uneasiness, discomfort, anger, shame, regret, sadness, or any other emotion that carries a negative charge.

6. Write down the names of two or three places or spaces, the thought of which provokes a feeling of uneasiness, discomfort, anger, shame, regret, sadness, or any other emotion that carries a negative charge.

7. Write down two or three issues that are unresolved for you, the thought of which provokes a feeling of uneasiness, discomfort, anger, shame, regret, sadness, or any other emotion that carries a negative charge.

8. Organize the "people," "places," and "issues" lists you just made, putting the people, places, or issues that hold the greatest charge or urgency at the top of the list and the ones carrying the least charge at the bottom.

9. Next to each relationship, place, or issue, note when and how you are going to create a change in order to clear the charge and clean things up.

10. Note next to each if there is anyone whose support you would like to enlist to help you to gain clarity and freedom around these relationships or issues.

11. If you know the first step to take in order to clear the issue or relationship, note it next to that item. If you don't know, next to that item schedule a place and time to focus on coming up with your first step.

12. Next to each issue and relationship, note the date by which you intend to be clear.

13. Write down the actions you have committed to and/or are on your calendar, allocating the time you need in your schedule.

____

____

____

____

____

____

____

____

____

14. Do what you need to do to follow through until you are clear and clean.

This practice becomes natural and automatic. The more you cultivate clear relationships, the easier it is to maintain this practice as a way of life. You'll find you feel lighter and have better interactions with others and greater conscious self-confidence!

Pivotal Point #2

Objective

To develop self-trust.

Activities

1. On a scale of 1 to 10, score your current level of self-trust.

   ☐1 ☐2 ☐3 ☐4 ☐5 ☐6 ☐7 ☐8 ☐9 ☐10

2. Identify three key strengths you know that you have, and write them down. Come up with a symbol to represent each one. Find something physical to represent each strength (such as an image, an item of jewelry or clothing, or an object from nature). You could paint, draw, or write something. Keep that representation close to you for a week where you can see, touch, or experience it in some way. Be intentional about recognizing these strengths.

   ____

   ____

   ____

3. Every day for one week, make a conscious choice to check inside yourself for your own opinion before asking anyone else for theirs and before discussing the matter with others.

4. Each day for one week, open a journal entry that begins with: "This is my opinion on . . ." Each day for one week, complete that sentence three times. Write in as much detail as possible, and free-flow without editing or rereading what you have written.

   This is my opinion on:

   ____

   ____

   This is my opinion on:

   ____

   ____

PIVOTAL POINTS

This is my opinion on:

This is my opinion on:

This is my opinion on:

This is my opinion on:

This is my opinion on:

5. Write a list of nine things you admire about yourself on any level. Keep your list close at hand and refer to it at least three times throughout your day. Read your list before going to sleep at night.

1.

2.

3.

4.

5.

6.

7.

8.

9.

PIVOTAL POINTS

Pivotal Point #3

Objective

To begin a healthy exercise routine.

Activities

Choose from one of two options, depending on the kind of exercise you prefer:

Option 1: Set your walking shoes out each night for one week. Wake a half hour earlier each day. Soon after waking, pull on your walking shoes and head out for a brisk half-hour walk. (Go to www.HotConfidence.com/energytools/walk_breathe_move/audio for your free download of my "Morning Walk, Breathing, and Gratitude Meditation.")

Option 2: Select a form of exercise that suits you, commit to it, and begin. Schedule at least three exercise slots per week. Remember to seek the advice of a medical professional or fitness trainer if you require guidance.

Pivotal Point #4

Objective

To strengthen your connection with nature.

Activities

1. Schedule a date with nature. Find a natural environment such as a beach, park, forest, river, or garden. You can do this exercise alone or share it with someone. Choose your time of day intentionally. You may wish to enjoy dawn, noon, or dusk, for example. (Whenever I can, I walk outside to be present with the sunset. This is my favorite time of day, when I can offer gratitude for the day's gifts and welcome the majesty of the night.) Your date can be as long or as short as suits you: ten minutes or a whole day. The idea is for you to get grounded and be fully present to your experience. Be with the sensations of your senses. Just be.

2. After your nature experience, do the following exercise using your journal or your *Hot Confidence Workbook* worksheet for Chapter 5 called "Reflections: Nature's Gift." List things that you learned and observed during the nature exercise, including at least one thing you learned about yourself.

REFLECTIONS: NATURE'S GIFT

This page is dedicated to the things I learned during my dates with nature.

3. Choose three of the following affirmations and repeat them three times each at least three times a day to embed these concepts in your life. (Of the affirmations you've been repeating from previous chapters, continue your regimen with the ones you find most potent and useful, and discontinue any that don't resonate with you. Update your Daily Affirmations and All-time Favorite Affirmations lists.)

I trust, love, and believe in myself wholly and completely.
All my relationships are clear, loving, and healthy.
Every day in every way my body becomes fitter and fitter.
Exercise gives me energy, positivity, and restful sleep.
I am connected with nature and with the entire universe.
All is well.

The following three affirmations can be repeated at night before you go to sleep:

I am safe, calm, and at peace.
Falling asleep and remaining asleep is easy and effortless.
I sleep deeply, profoundly, and peacefully, waking rested, relaxed, and refreshed. As I sleep, my heart radiates joy and my body restores and repairs, so that I wake refreshed and ready to start a new day.

6

Activate Your Attraction Engine

"The Soul should always stand ajar. Ready to welcome the ecstatic experience."

~ Emily Dickinson

Let's acknowledge and celebrate your magnetic movement toward your magnificence. By now your strong foundation is set in place. You have discovered how to ground yourself, get present, take care of the Four Confidence Columns, and strengthen your self-trust. It's time to reveal the tips, techniques, and exercises that will help you fully and playfully experience pleasure, passion, and creative potency so that you can unleash your unique charisma.

Let your hair down and enjoy your ride to irresistible!

It's possible that although you may be experiencing some external success, you are still (secretly) unsure of who you are. In order to connect with your potential, we'll begin with where you are now.

1. Circle the phrases that describe you:

    - I feel and share deep emotion
    - I move with fluidity
    - I have and share great sensitivity
    - I enjoy a passion for life
    - I take joy in the five senses
    - I am inspired with creative ideas
    - I engage in creative projects
    - I enjoy sexual pleasure

2. For each of the above, give yourself a score between 1 and 10, where 1 is "almost none" and 10 is "off the charts." Now give yourself a score for each in terms of where you'd like to be once your confidence and self-esteem levels are consistently high.

- I feel and share deep emotion
  ☐1 ☐2 ☐3 ☐4 ☐5 ☐6 ☐7 ☐8 ☐9 ☐10
- I move with fluidity
  ☐1 ☐2 ☐3 ☐4 ☐5 ☐6 ☐7 ☐8 ☐9 ☐10
- I have and share great sensitivity
  ☐1 ☐2 ☐3 ☐4 ☐5 ☐6 ☐7 ☐8 ☐9 ☐10
- I enjoy a passion for life
  ☐1 ☐2 ☐3 ☐4 ☐5 ☐6 ☐7 ☐8 ☐9 ☐10
- I take joy in the five senses
  ☐1 ☐2 ☐3 ☐4 ☐5 ☐6 ☐7 ☐8 ☐9 ☐10
- I am inspired with creative ideas
  ☐1 ☐2 ☐3 ☐4 ☐5 ☐6 ☐7 ☐8 ☐9 ☐10
- I engage in creative projects
  ☐1 ☐2 ☐3 ☐4 ☐5 ☐6 ☐7 ☐8 ☐9 ☐10
- I enjoy sexual pleasure
  ☐1 ☐2 ☐3 ☐4 ☐5 ☐6 ☐7 ☐8 ☐9 ☐10

Deciphering your scores

If you score a composite rating of seven or above in the first scoring, it means that between the sixth and twenty-fourth month of your infancy you experienced warmth, closeness, and connection. At that time you developed a sensate connection between your inner and outer world in a supportive environment.

If you scored below seven, take heart. By working with the tools you learn in *Hot Confidence*, your *Hot Confidence Workbook*, and *Heart and Soul of Confidence*, you can rewrite the impressions from your past, unlocking the power of your second chakra, and of every chakra.

Exploring Your Essential Polarities

All life and the very structure of experience involve polarities and duality. Ask yourself:

"What opposing forces do I need to bring together in order to . . . ?"

1. Have Hot Confidence
2. Be happy
3. Be successful in business
4. Attract my soul mate
5. Enjoy wealth
6. Balance the second chakra
7. Create the difference I am alive at this time to make

THE POWER OF *GIVE* AND THE SPIRITUALITY OF *TAKE*

The secret to experiencing grace in abundance is your ability to be clear and to put into words precisely what you would like to receive in all areas of your life and exactly what you are willing to give. Allow yourself a full half hour for each of the two parts of this process. The results will astound you if you attend to this with your fullest intention, imagination, and heart.

What would you like to receive?

Consider what you would like to receive in your relationships, in your work, and in your life. Give yourself the gift of putting it into words. In your mind's eye, create images depicting exactly what you would like to bring in. Write your answers to this important question below. Add today's date to this declaration.

What would you like to give?

If you could give anything to anyone, what would you most like to give? See yourself, in your imagination, fulfilling that giving and surpassing your expectations of what you are able to share. Put your thoughts into words below. Add today's date your declaration.

Are You Ready to Dare to Be Hot?

Svadhistana, the second chakra, governs the energy of attraction and creativity and is the reservoir of your sexual energy.

The eight qualities that equate with a balanced, robust second chakra will give you the zest and backbone to be confident and alluring.

Write a Self-Commitment Action Statement to improve each area, below each quality listed below, in which you agree to take action within the next twenty-four hours. Your actions can be as simple and practical as you need them to be. Follow through on your Self-Commitment Action Statements and you will notice immediate, powerful transformation in your life as you become more creative, happier, and command more respect from others.

1. Emotional intelligence, clarity, and steadiness

2. Enjoyment of life

3. Comfortableness with sex and intimacy

4. Appreciation of the pleasures of all five senses

5. Clear establishment of boundaries with others, including sexual boundaries

6. Inner flexibility—the capacity to accept movement and change

7. Capacity to feel deeply without having to be dramatic

8. Nurturing of self and others through maintaining health

After implementing your Self-Commitment Action Statements for seven days, write down at least three key learnings below:

1.
2.
3.
4.
5.
6.
7.
8.
9.

By applying yourself to becoming more at ease with movement, intimacy, change, sensuality, sexuality, and enjoyment of life, your sense of autonomy in the world grows. As you become more competent you become more confident.

The Pivotal Points section will guide you to liberating the life force of your first and second chakras and help you take charge of your own power of attraction.

Pivotal Points

What you'll need

1. *An uninterrupted space*
2. *A pen and your journal (optional)*
3. *Water to sip*

Pivotal Point #1

Objective

To discover the environment in which your beliefs around pleasure were established.

Special Note: This exercise may trigger uncomfortable memories and awareness. Please seek the support of a carefully chosen professional (such as a coach, mentor, therapist, healer) or a trusted friend to take best care of your self. Remember to do this exercise from a place of self-respect, compassion and curiosity.

Activities

1. Ask the questions that follow the list below and write down your answers as they relate to each of the these people:

    - Your mother (or the person who mothered you)
    - Your father (or whoever was the father-figure in your home until you turned seven)
    - Each of your siblings
    - Your grandmothers
    - Your grandfathers
    - Any other significant caregivers
    - Teachers
    - People from your childhood who spring to mind who had an influence on you.

If your memory is flexible enough, you may be able to retrieve experiences from as far back as when you were six months old. Your unconscious mind is infinitely wise, and you have all the information within you—work with the answers that come up for you in a respectful and curious way. Remember that your unconscious responses were formed by many influences. Approach your inner reflections with interest and without judgment or attachment.

PIVOTAL POINTS

You can copy these questions for each of the people listed above, or complete the exercise in your journal.

MOTHER

1. How did this person relate to pleasure?
2. Did this person express pleasure?
3. What words did they use in expressing pleasure?
4. What actions did they take in expressing pleasure?
5. How did they encourage pleasure in the home?
6. How did they discourage pleasure in the home?
7. Did this person play with you?
8. Did this person encourage you to play?
9. What was this person's attitude toward touch?
10. Did this person cuddle you?
11. Did this person express pleasure to you verbally?
12. Did this person validate your own experiences of pleasure?

FATHER

1. How did this person relate to pleasure?
2. Did this person express pleasure?
3. What words did they use in expressing pleasure?
4. What actions did they take in expressing pleasure?
5. How did they encourage pleasure in the home?

6. How did they discourage pleasure in the home?

7. Did this person play with you?

8. Did this person encourage you to play?

9. What was this person's attitude toward touch?

10. Did this person cuddle you?

11. Did this person express pleasure to you verbally?

12. Did this person validate your own experiences of pleasure?

SIBLINGS

1. How did this person relate to pleasure?

2. Did this person express pleasure?

3. What words did they use in expressing pleasure?

4. What actions did they take in expressing pleasure?

5. How did they encourage pleasure in the home?

6. How did they discourage pleasure in the home?

7. Did this person play with you?

8. Did this person encourage you to play?

9. What was this person's attitude toward touch?

10. Did this person cuddle you?

11. Did this person express pleasure to you verbally?

12. Did this person validate your own experiences of pleasure?

PIVOTAL POINT #2

Objective

To support the steady and ongoing development of your confidence through the unique expression of your creativity.

Activities

1. Do something creative every day for the next seven days and, before you go to sleep, reflect on these experiences on your Reflections: Creativity and Me Today worksheet (You'll find your worksheet at the end of this chapter). Write about what impact your effort made on you and others.

2. Find something creative to do that is new for you. Try at least three different things over the next week. Possibilities include learning a craft or skill, playing a musical instrument, cooking something new, painting or drawing, writing a story, joining a choir, taking a dance class, or any other new creative activity that appeals to you. The options are endless. Remember: "Just do it" in your judgment-free zone.

PIVOTAL POINT #3

Objective

To know the order of your Six Core Needs, identifying the two that are most important to you.

Note: Refer to Hot Confidence *for details.*

There's an emotional side to everything we do. Healthy pleasure brings satisfaction, while addictive pleasure brings only a craving for more. Without consciousness, reactions are ruled by emotion.

Behavior naturally attempts to find fulfillment and is driven by what Tony Robbins refers to as the Six Core Needs.

You must understand these needs, and identify your top two, in order to know yourself and what drives you. If you can identify your top drivers, then you gain control and choice. This ensures you can meet your core needs and express them in ways that are supportive of your well-being, personal mission, and vision.

The **Six Core Needs**, as defined by Tony Robbins, are:

- Certainty
- Uncertainty/Variety
- Significance
- Love and Connection
- Growth
- Contribution

Certainty, for most people, equates with survival. It is about avoiding pain and gaining the pleasure that comes of stability, predictability, order, and steadiness. Certainty is the need for control, safety, and comfort.

Uncertainty or **variety** relates to a profound need for change, choices, and movement, such as travel or work that offers flexible time, diversity, and a whole array of experiences and projects. Uncertainty is the need for spontaneity, excitement, and adventure.

Significance refers to the need to feel important and that your life counts for something.

Connection is the need to belong, to be understood and to understand, to give and receive love.

Growth is the need to become all that you can be (an essential requirement for personal development).

Contribution is the need to give back, to contribute outside of yourself. Contribution gives life heightened meaning.

Activities

1. The table below lists the Six Core Needs with spaces underneath. Score yourself on a scale of 1 to 10 for how important each need is in your life (1 being "not important," 10 being "very important"). From these scores, identify your top two needs. They will be the two you ranked with scores closest to ten. These are the needs that must be met in order for you to feel fulfilled and happy. Next, list the order of the Six Core Needs in your life, based on the marks you gave them.

   If this is confusing, consider this example: Lucy gave *certainty* an 8, *variety* a 3, *significance* a 9, *love and connection* an 8, *growth* a 7, and *contribution* an 8. This tells us her top core need is *significance*. Although she scored *certainty*, *contribution*, and *love and connection* all as 8s,

when she looked at her life she could easily see that the need for *love and connection* was even more critical to her than the other two. Then she ordered her list of the Six Core Needs in terms of their importance to her personally, and came up with this: (1) Significance, (2) Love and Connection, (3) Certainty, (4) Contribution, (5) Growth, (6) Variety.

Certainty	*Variety*	*Significance*	*Love and Connection*	*Growth*	*Contribution*

My Core Needs in Order:

1.____________________________________

2.____________________________________

3.____________________________________

4.____________________________________

5.____________________________________

6.____________________________________

2. Think of something you love to do. Does it help meet all or some of your needs? Which ones? (The things we love to do the most usually fulfill multiple needs.) Think of another activity you greatly enjoy and ask yourself the same questions about it. Write your answers below.

Note: Some and not all of your needs may be met. That's fine.

1.____________________________________

2.____________________________________

3.____________________________________

4.____________________________________

5.____________________________________

6.____________________________________

3. Think of a "story" you have about yourself (where "story" is the meaning you have given to an experience—an interpretation of reality)—that limits you and burdens you. Ask yourself what needs are being met through telling yourself and/or others this story.

   Write down what needs are being met:

   1.____

   2.____

   3.____

   4.____

   Is it time to give it up?

   What do you need to do to make a shift?

   What new behaviors, beliefs, or thoughts do you need to replace it with?

PIVOTAL POINT #4

Objective

To connect with the power of give and the spirituality of take; to harmonize and revitalize the polarities, bringing greater wealth, confidence, fulfillment, happiness, and meaning into your life

Activities

1. Create your list of the things that replenish you.

PIVOTAL POINTS

2. Think of someone you admire or are inspired by. What are the ways they give or contribute? Now put yourself in their shoes, and from their perspective answer, "What replenishes you?" Write down your answers.

3. Select items and actions from the list in (2) to add to your own list. You are welcome to borrow items from my list that I shared in this chapter of *Hot Confidence*.

4. Commit to experiencing at least one of the replenishment items or actions on your list each day.

5. Keep your list within easy access, dipping into it for ideas when you feel you need replenishing—or just for fun!

6. What would you like to receive in your relationships? In your work? In your life? Give yourself the gift of putting that into words. Close your eyes and let yourself imagine, in your mind's eye, the symbols,

PIVOTAL POINTS

concepts, pictures, words, or scenarios that depict what you'd like to have.

7. Now write, draw, or paint your answer to (6). Do this exercise every quarter at the beginning of spring, summer, fall, and winter.

8. What would you like to give? If you could give anything to anyone at anytime, what would you most like to give? Close your eyes and see yourself, in your mind's eye, fulfilling that giving and surpassing your expectations with what you are able to share.

9. Now write, draw, or paint your answer to (8). Do this exercise every quarter at the beginning of spring, summer, fall, and winter.

PIVOTAL POINTS

Pivotal Point #5

Objective

To familiarize yourself with what pleases you; to extend your range of pleasure and create positive, personal-sense reference points, building self-respect and confidence in this area.

Activities

1. Find three sensual ways to enjoy pleasure each day for the next week. Here are a few ideas: savoring a superb meal, relaxing in a bath with essential oils, getting a massage, walking barefoot on the beach, having a manicure, listening to music by candlelight, taking a sunbath, reading poetry, snuggling with your cat, watching a great movie, going to a play or concert, visiting an art museum, sitting quietly in your garden. Brainstorm for a few minutes, listing other pleasure-giving activities you can think of. Then enjoy some of them!

2. Choose three of the following affirmations and repeat each one three times at least three times a day to embed these concepts in your life. (Of the affirmations you've been repeating from previous chapters, continue your regimen with the ones you find most potent and useful, and discontinue any that don't resonate with you. Update your Daily Affirmations and All-time Favorite Affirmations lists at the end of this workbook.)

I appreciate, nourish, and celebrate pleasure in my life.
I am sacredly connected with my sexuality.
I am open to receiving wisdom and information from my feelings.
I welcome the power in my presence as I boldly give and receive.
I move effortlessly with flexibility, ease, and grace.
I enjoy my life more and more each day.
My divine evolution as an aware, sensual individual is a joyous gift to the universe.

REFLECTIONS: CREATIVITY AND ME TODAY

Date: ____________________

Write about what impact your creative effort made on you and others.

Note the creative things you did today, and how that impacted your life and the lives of others.

These questions will guide you:

What did you enjoy?

What did you find challenging?

What would you do more of?

What did you learn?

How did this enrich your life?

How did this creative activity touch the life of another/others?

7
THE CALL TO COMMAND

"I think of life itself now as a wonderful play that I've written for myself, and so my purpose is to have the utmost fun playing my part."

~ Shirley MacLaine

The focus of this chapter is how to build resolute self-esteem to ignite your mojo, strike up your momentum, and energize your magnificence. You'll figure out how to create your autonomy, your individuation, and your authenticity.

Make the techniques and exercises in this chapter your own by embracing this value-rich content fully and actively. Do all of the processes suggested in these pages and in *Hot Confidence* to give yourself the most potent opportunity to become and express your full self in the world.

You will discover the Five Core-Drivers of Self-Esteem and the indicators of high self-esteem, learn the seven strategies for creating sizzling self-esteem, unpack shame, and meet with *manipura*, the third chakra—your command center.

Your results will depend on how much intentional action you take and how much you're willing to put into your growth.

"Wherever you go, go with all your heart."

~ Confucius

Let's set the scene by asking you to consider these questions. Write your answers below:

- Can you relate to giving your power away to others?
- Do you define yourself in terms of what is expected of you?
- Have you lost your sense of spontaneity or playfulness?
- Do you distrust your own abilities and fear the consequences of your own energy?
- Do you ever feel constricted and self-conscious?
- Are you unable to trust your basic impulses or feelings?
- Do you constantly monitor your thoughts and the emotions that come from deep inside you?

If you answered yes to all or most of these questions, your self-esteem is low. The good news is that you can learn, develop, and improve your self-esteem by returning to *Hot Confidence* generally—in particular Chapter 7—and by completing the processes right here in your *Hot Confidence Workbook* so that you can:

1. Enjoy your life
2. Be increasingly certain that you *can* create stability
3. Feel enthusiastic and optimistic
4. Have energetic vitality
5. Have a sense of personal power and inner strength
6. Approach life as an adventure to be lived to the fullest
7. Take action, engaging in activities and dealing with the world
8. Maintain your direction and progress, even when challenged
9. Be proactive and embrace obstacles with flexibility
10. Be willing to take considered risks, explore the unknown, and make mistakes
11. Take responsibility for your life (self-owned, self-led)

All of these qualities and strengths combine in healthy self-esteem and indicate a robust and balanced third chakra, or solar plexus.

If you have the sense that part of you wants to grow, shine, and be the amazing person you know you can be, while another part is hiding away, ashamed, blaming, doubting, and fearful, then give yourself the profound gift of scheduling time and creating the space in your life to engage with the material in this chapter. Step into this important section with curiosity, commitment, and compassion for the exciting unfolding of your quest for the brightest, authentic expression of yourself in the world. It *is* your time to choose self-command. Let's do this, together. I believe in the astonishing light you are.

Here are the practical tools that, along with the guidance in *Hot Confidence,* provide your recovery regimen to put you at the helm of your optimistic, proactive, self-defined journey so that you can master your life, shape your destiny, and have fun!

The "Radiant Full-Life Framework"

The "Radiant Full-Life Framework" helps you identify the areas in your life in which low self-esteem holds you back, and reveals clearly where you can focus to create contentment, health, and your success.

Towards the end of 2010, in the early hours of the morning, I woke with the vision of every person's life—be they alive or already passed on—represented as a radiant, dynamic star in a vast galaxy of pulsing lights in a universe of midnight-blue potentiality. I had gone to sleep with the intention of waking up with a clear, easy formula for integrating the different areas that make up a life. I wanted my model to reflect the constantly moving nature of being, how priorities and perspectives shift, and the effect of a change in one aspect of life on the whole. Before dawn broke, I had mapped out the structure and process I gift to you here, titled the "Radiant Full-Life Framework," so that you can follow a simple method to see your life as it is, create what you want, and make adjustments along the way as you evolve into your magnificent self.

Objective

To familiarize you with your "Radiant Full-Life Framework" so you can easily evaluate yourself in the main areas of your life to reveal what you need to pay attention to in order to strengthen your self-esteem.

In addition to the straight-forward, yet stellar structure of the framework, you'll find that I have distilled the essential elements for a full life, mapped it out into sections, and provided the five core questions to ask yourself at each point and the five key principles to navigate by. All you have to do is schedule time and space to reflect and set your intentions.

THE RADIANT FULL-LIFE FRAMEWORK

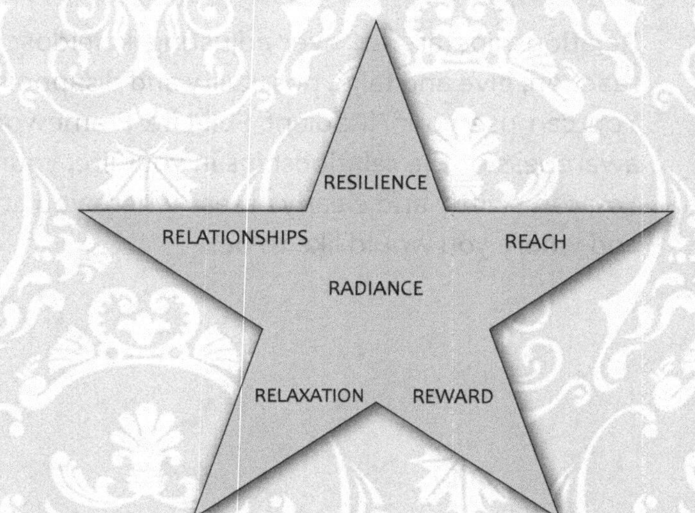

The six overarching categories that make up your "Radiant Full-Life Framework" are:

1. Resilience
2. Relationships
3. Reach
4. Reward
5. Relaxation
6. Radiance

1. ***Resilience*** refers to your health. It includes your general health, your mental health, your emotional health, and your physical health. When you are evaluating your health in each of these areas, both as it is and how you would like it to be, consider:

   a. Your attitude to it
   b. How you nourish yourself in this area
   c. Your practice—what actions you take in terms of the specific area of health

   By evaluating your resilience (health) in this level of detail you are able to quickly discern where you need to make changes to improve your resilience. Can you appreciate how making positive shifts in these areas, however small, would affect every other area and the sum total of the interplay of every aspect, which I call your Radiance?

2. ***Relationships.*** You are already aware of how important relationships are in the scheme of having a fulfilled life. Clear relationships are one of the Four Confidence Columns you discovered in Chapter 5 of *Hot Confidence*.

   Relationships are an ever-adjusting kaleidoscope of initiation and reaction, give and take, possibility and disappointment, loss and love. You can use your "Radiant Full-Life Framework" to heighten your awareness of the relationships in your life, your work, and your play. You can swiftly and clearly assess where you are in your interactions and where you would like to be.

Note: When you measure where you are and where you would like to be with your relationships, be practical, honest, and realistic. There is no right, no wrong, and nothing to prove here. Have it the way you want it to be. For example, as a result of the way my life panned out, the healthy scale of interaction for me with my mother would make a 7 out of 10 of the very best and most honest intention I have for this relationship. If I pressured myself to achieve a 10 in this relationship, my evaluation would serve as something that in this moment I cannot see myself achieving. It is not realistic. For where my mother and I are in our lives, and with the past as it was, I am joyful when I achieve a pure 7. I trust this makes sense.

The idea of ranking by number is to provide a scale for comparison and improvement; it's not a beat-up stick! Remember: I have a "no-self-beat-up rule," Please live by this rule.

On the "Radiant Full-Life Framework Self-Evaluation and Visioning" worksheet below you'll see the following relationships listed: your relationship with yourself, the Divine, your partner (your primary intimate partner; if you want to bring your soul mate into your life, you would indicate this on your worksheet), your animals or pets, your mother, your father, your family (list your family members and rate each relationship separately), your friends, your associates, and the people with whom you'd like to have relationships.

3. ***Reach.*** In the "Radiant Full-Life Framework," your ***Reach*** includes your education and learning, spiritual growth, and contribution and giving to the world.

4. ***Reward*** refers to your finance, your business or means of earning a living, and the gifts, miracles, collaboration, and surprises that come your way. By making gifts, miracles, collaboration, and surprises overt and conscious, you are creating a space for rewards to come your way in many forms.

5. ***Relaxation.*** Any activity or pursuit that brings you relaxation can be added to this category. I have included in the evaluation worksheet adventure, travel, pampering, entertainment, reading, meditation, and exercise. Examples you might add for yourself are time to dream, socializing, meals out, theater, shopping, martial arts, painting, singing, dance.

6. ***Radiance*** is made up of the dynamic interplay of the other five categories, and is the vitality, magnificence, and quality of light you bring to the universe by being you at any moment.

THE "RADIANT FULL-LIFE FRAMEWORK"

In the table below, rank yourself on a scale of 1 to 10
(1 is very low and 10 is outstanding) from these two perspectives:

1. Where you are now in your life
2. Where you would like to be

Note: There is no "right" or "wrong" answer. Your scale of evaluation is for your increased self-knowledge. Ask your unconscious mind to be fully present, accepting the first number that comes up for you.

	Your Radiant Full-Life Framework Self-Evaluation & Visioning	Out of 10	
1. Resilience		a	b
	Health: Overall		
	Attitude (Mindset)		
	Nourishment (Diet)		
	Practice (Fitness)		
	Mental:		
	Attitude (Mindset)		
	Nourishment (Diet)		
	Practice (Fitness)		
	Emotional:		
	Attitude (Mindset)		
	Nourishment (Diet)		

	Your Radiant Full-Life Framework Self-Evaluation & Visioning	Out of 10	
	Practice (Fitness)		
	Physical:		
	Attitude (Mindset)		
	Nourishment (Diet)		
	Practice (Fitness)		
2. Relationships	**Self**		
	God/The Divine		
	Partner: Personal Primary/Intimate		
	Animals/Pets		
	Family: Overall		
	List your family members and rate each relationships separately		
	Mother		
	Father		

	Your Radiant Full-Life Framework Self-Evaluation & Visioning	Out of 10	
	Friends		
	List your main 3-7 friends and rate each relationship separately		
	Associates		
	List the relationships that matter to you with people you know or who have an influence in your life. These could include work relationships with your colleagues, boss, secretary, fellow workers, etc.		
	People I would like to have a relationship with		

	Your Radiant Full-Life Framework Self-Evaluation & Visioning	Out of 10	
3. Reach			
	Education/Learning Your learning may be through formal study with a school, university, or other institution, or it may be informal through reading, research, online programs, belonging to an interest group, and so on.		
	Spiritual Growth Do you meditate or attend any form of spiritual development group in your community, circle, synagogue, church, coven, religious institution, and so on?		
	Contribution/Giving Are you adding value to your world, community, or family? Are you volunteering, teaching, or sharing your gifts in any way?		
4. Reward			
	Finance Refers to your level of income, your money management, your investments		
	Business Your means of earning a living		

	Your Radiant Full-Life Framework Self-Evaluation & Visioning	Out of 10	
	Potential and Gifts This is your open space for welcoming reward in any energetic form and can include time, exchange in the form of service or goods, ideas, support, or miracles.		
5. Relaxation			
	Adventure		
	Travel		
	Pampering		
	Entertainment		
	Reading		
	Meditation		
	Exercise		

Now it's time to do some detailed, intentional visioning and planning in each category.

You can apply your "Radiant Full-Life Framework" whenever you feel it is in your interest to set some new goals, milestones, or visions for yourself. This may be as often as once a week. (I have a date with myself every Sunday night to set up the week, at which time I do an evaluation using this exact form. I also apply my "Radiant Full-Life Framework" in setting up each quarter of the year and for creating the most outstanding year yet, at the end of the year.) Give it a red-hot go so that you can start enjoying the results that speed in!

The Shame Serpent

In *Hot Confidence*, you can review the way the shame cycle perpetuates itself, causing your inherent optimism, hope, and free-flowing energy to become trapped and subverted. Remember, the focus of your serpent is to block effective action, limit your spontaneity, and mind-control you and your basic instincts.

In the list below, put a circle around any of the following that are true for you:

- You feel stuck.
- You honor your thoughts more than your instincts.
- You constantly hear voices in your head telling you how inferior and worthless you are.
- You experience constant negative self-talk.
- You fall into patterns of compulsive repetition and addiction.
- You sabotage your work and success by procrastinating and other passive-aggressive behaviors.
- You binge or resort to substance abuse.
- You fill in this one: ______________________________

Remind yourself that you are experiencing any of the above because as a very young child you couldn't explain behavior in terms of parental or adult shortcomings, so unconsciously you came to the conclusion that you were at fault. It is highly likely that you experienced any of the following or a combination:

- Assignment of age-inappropriate responsibility
- Misuse of authority (including being spoken to without respect)
- Neglect
- Abandonment
- Sexual abuse
- Emotional abuse
- Physical abuse
- Verbal abuse (including excessive criticism)s

And so your shame serpent was conceived. Refer to *Hot Confidence*, Chapter 7, for a deeper understanding, and review the section titled, "Mastering Your Shame Serpent" for solutions and suggestions. This section is followed by eleven practical strategies for balancing and supercharging your third chakra so that you can achieve your optimum state of vitality and strong connection with yourself.

MOMENTS OF TRIUMPH

Focusing on your successes attracts more of the same! Add Your Moments of Triumph to this page daily to build up your own silo of special moments. Celebrate and acknowledge any wins you have had (big or small). Writing them down creates awareness and encourages you to recognize your achievements as you continue to progress toward the glowing results you're bringing in. This page is your personal positive resource for now and for years to come. Duplicate this page as required.

Acknowledging and celebrating your successes is one major way to strengthen your self-esteem.

List three moments of triumph from your day below. You can celebrate and acknowledge any wins you have had (big or small). If you can't think of anything from today in particular, pick three moments from your life.

1.____

2.____

3.____

Add these to your worksheet titled Moments of Triumph. You'll find this worksheet at the end of the chapter.

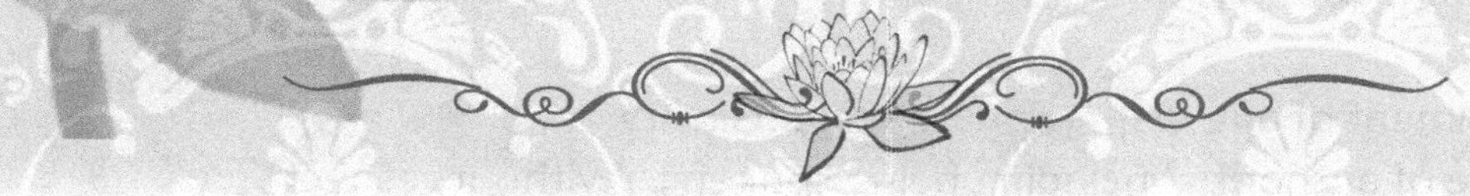

In Chapter 7 of *Hot Confidence*, you will have developed a deep appreciation for the influences that shaped your relationship with your personal power. You've met manipura, the lustrous gem of your solar plexus. To strengthen and maintain your inner call to command so that you integrate your significant findings about yourself and your self-esteem, complete the Pivotal Points section below.

PIVOTAL POINTS

PIVOTAL POINTS

What you'll need

1. *An uninterrupted space*
2. *A pen and your journal (optional)*
3. *Water to sip*

PIVOTAL POINT #1

Objective

To distinguish between factors that negatively influence your self-esteem and those that nurture it.

Activities

1. Think of your self-esteem as a reservoir contained by shores and a dam. If you'd rather come up with your own image of a holding vessel, please do (it might be a vat, tank, crate, or truck, for instance). See your self-esteem as this holding vessel. When it is between 75 and 95 percent full, your self-esteem and self-appraisal are healthy and resourceful. When your reservoir is running anywhere below 55 percent full, you're in a red-alert region where you'll be feeling challenged.

   Now calibrate your reservoir.

   What was your self-esteem level before you began reading this book?

   What was it at the beginning of Chapter 7?

   Where is it now?

   ____

   ____

   ____

2. What makes your life parched? What makes it barren? What makes your self-esteem run dry; your reservoir run out? Identify at least three situations, three experiences, and three attitudes that deplete your self-esteem.

   ____

   ____

3. List three ways you speak to yourself that bring on "drought."

4. What are the drops of rain in your life that fill your reservoir? List five things that increase your self-esteem.

5. What causes your self-esteem to overflow and flood? (When self-esteem overflows into the domain of arrogance, that is not resourceful. There is a place of balance in framing self-esteem.)

6. What's the first and easiest thing you can do right now to replenish your self-esteem reservoir?

7. Take action within the next twenty-four hours.

PIVOTAL POINTS

PIVOTAL POINT #2

Objective

To understand authority's influence in your life and to reclaim your personal command.

Activities

1. Write down your answers to the following questions:

   a. Who was the central authority figure in your life during your childhood?

   b. By what manner and means did they establish their authority?

   c. How did you feel about their authority? Did you obey out of respect, fear, or desire for approval—or a combination of these? If a combination, what was the combination?

   d. How did you react to authority as a child? Did you mostly rebel against authority or obey it?

   e. How do you react to authority today?

   f. If you react to authority in various ways, what are the circumstances that affect how you react?

PIVOTAL POINTS

2. Describe your sense of your "inner authority." Where is it right now? What are you telling yourself as you think "inner authority"? Are any sounds, images, or physical sensations associated with inner authority for you?

3. Who is your inner authority modeled on or inspired by?

4. Does your inner authority respect your physical, emotional, and mental limitations?

5. Does your inner authority appreciate your need for expansion and growth?

6. Does your inner authority respect your sense of self?

7. What nourishes and strengthens your inner authority?

8. What would be the motto of your inner authority?

9. How can your inner authority align more effectively with your need to support the outcomes you want on all levels of your life?

PIVOTAL POINT #3

Objective

To build your positive reference points for outstanding self-esteem and Hot Confidence.

Activities

1. Before you go to bed each night, identify three triumphant moments from your life or from your day. Ideally, share these with someone who will appreciate and celebrate them with you. Write your moments in your journal or *Hot Confidence Workbook*, turning to your Chapter 7 worksheet: "Moments of Triumph."

2. Choose three of the following affirmations and repeat each one three times at least three times a day to embed these concepts in your life. (Of the affirmations you've been repeating from previous chapters, continue your regimen with the ones you find most potent and useful, and discontinue any that don't resonate with you. Update your Daily Affirmations and All-time Favorite Affirmations lists at the end of this workbook.)

PIVOTAL POINTS

I honor my authentic self; I celebrate my uniqueness, standing tall in my own authority.
I decide. I can do whatever I intend to do.
I joyfully take care of my needs and responsibilities.
My positive self-image improves each day.
I surround myself with inspiring people and foster clear, loving relationships.
My confidence and self-esteem grow as I share my unique gifts with competence, awareness, and certainty.
My spirituality and connectedness support, serve, and sustain my healthy self-esteem.
I celebrate my right to be an individual and express my uniqueness.
I have all the courage, strength, and optimism I need within me now.
I am proactive, positive, and powerful.

PIVOTAL POINTS

Moments of Triumph

List your moments of triumph here. Keep adding your successes to this page however large or small you perceive them to be. This practice will help you become more aware of your wins. Quite rapidly you'll start to notice how you experience an increasing number of moments of triumphs. It is true that what you focus on you get!

My Daily Affirmations

My All-time Favorite Affirmations

Moving Forward:
Your Thoughts

1. These are the three most significant things I learned about myself through my *Hot Confidence* journey so far:

   a.____

   b.____

   c.____

2. These are the three ways I have transformed most:

   a.____

   b.____

   c.____

3. This is now what I know to be true about myself:

4. This is the action I feel uncomfortable to take, and I commit to doing: (Write down the date by which you will have taken action.)

5. When I find myself uncertain, this is what I will say to myself to remind myself of my own resourcefulness, power, and choices:

6. This is what I celebrate about myself today:

Moving Forward: Shine Your Light

"Life isn't about finding yourself. Life is about creating yourself."

~ George Bernard Shaw

Congratulations! If you've given yourself the gift of making the commitment to your journey of self-discovery, you've already made a difference to yourself and others. Thank you for investing in yourself by taking your time and energy to do this most profound personal work, building your confidence and self-esteem, and so becoming more of your authentic self.

Developing confidence and self-esteem, like life, is not linear. The dragon and the shame serpent strike, lash, and rest in their own rhythm. As your awareness grows, their ancient dance becomes a moving evolution toward new horizons, gathering new perspectives all the way. That is the dedication of this workbook.

You have dared to dance! You now know you have a song worth listening to. You can appreciate your value, and you believe in yourself even more. As you take your light out into the world and experience the evidence of your successes, you can attract the relationships and opportunities you desire.

If you followed along and you're still with me, you've built a firm foundation from which to progress for your success, health, and happiness. Refer to this workbook, over and over again, and to *Hot Confidence,* when you need to remind yourself that you can change anything you choose to.

Delve deeply into these resources to connect constantly with your purpose and your core needs so that you remain on track and in alignment with your true self. You can energize your self-esteem reservoir and supercharge your confidence by revisiting the exercises outlined in these pages.

It is no coincidence that you are alive during this exciting time of rapid transformation on this fragile and abundant planet. Bring into being the creations of your passion.

"Today you are You, that is truer than true. There is no-one alive who is Youer than You."

~ Dr. Seuss, *Happy Birthday to You*

I honor the circumstances that conspired to bring you to these pages, and joyfully respect your unique reasons for continuing to pursue your self-growth. Seek out the *Heart and Soul of Confidence* and your *Heart and Soul of Confidence Workbook* so that you can discover, clarify, and fulfill your divine assignment, creating even more confidence for yourself.

Perhaps, if someone else crosses your path who wants to overcome shame, fear, and self-doubt, you'll pass on *Hot Confidence* so that they, too, can learn ways to reconnect with their forgotten dreams and share in these strategies for positive transformation.

"When there is light in the soul, there will be beauty in the person.
When there is beauty in the person, there is harmony in the house.
When there is harmony in the house, there will be order in the nation.
When there is order in the nation, there will be peace in the world."

~ Chinese Proverb

You are right here, on the *Hot Confidence* trail, because it's your time to be fully *you* and to live into your magnificent potential. As you become more resilient, may your heart fill with love and know peace.

At this topsy-turvy time of transition in the evolvement of our planet, when change is making itself felt in every area of life, your distinct contribution to your family and your community becomes more important by the minute. In a world in which two hundred species are becoming extinct each day, it's more important than ever before to shine your light.

Stepping out to stand up for who you are began with your quest to face your fears and overcome your shame, doubt, and self-defeating behaviors. You've discovered that self-esteem can be learned, and you've found out how to develop different communication strategies. Well done! By doing so, you enrich the world with your strengths, which inspires others to do the same. Keep applying the tools, techniques, and strategies revealed to you.

I trust that you'll appreciate by now that living Hot Confidence has something to do with the value you can bring to your loved ones, your community, and our planet. You're ready to make the shift from what I call *integral confidence,* which is governed by the core physical components that have constituted the subject matter of this book, to *influential confidence.*

Influential confidence is ruled by the heart, mind, and spirit, and has to do with the authentic alignment of your actions with your message and higher purpose. This is the subject matter of *The Heart and Soul of Confidence*, the metaphysical companion and follow-up volume to *Hot Confidence: Conscious Pathways to Take You from Mini-Me to Magnificent.*

You have taken action. You're in the tiny percentile of individuals who follow through. Well done! As you take bold steps toward becoming the extraordinary person you know yourself to be, you'll find opportunities, relationships, and possibilities opening to receive you and propel you on your way for good.

Hot Confidence and your *Hot Confidence Workbook* have given you practical ways to engage and build your self-belief. The *Heart and Soul of Confidence* is this book's metaphysical companion. We'll pick up at the solar plexus and head upward to the higher chakras for an uplifting exploration into the spirit, mindset, and emotions of confidence, so that your purpose, passion, and prosperity are aligned for your benefit and the greater good of others.

I sincerely appreciate the positive transformation you have already made by your commitment to yourself. You are constructively doing, reflecting, and connecting. I see your light.

Love who you are. Love what you do. Love creating your magnificent difference. We'll meet again soon.

Conspiring for your success and happiness with
love, light, and inspiration,

Nadine Love

How to Reach Me

For inquiries about *Hot Confidence* and *Create Your Difference* workshops, seminars, and mentoring, or to contact me about my products, books, and services, visit my website at www.NadineLove.com where you'll find a contact form that comes directly to me.

A Note to Mentors, Coaches, Therapists, Trainers, Teachers, and Human Resource Professionals

Thank you for sharing the stories, techniques, and strategies that are the conscious pathways to take your clients and students from mini-me to magnificent. You do wonderful work in an important and often challenging profession. Take the very best care of yourselves in your own quests to find health, happiness, and your magnificence. In so doing, you continue to inspire others.

About the Author

Nadine Love is a prizewinning transformational author, celebrated international speaker, award-winning trainer, and motivational mentor. With twenty-five years' experience in the international wellness industry, she is acclaimed for facilitating deep, rapid, and lasting change with groups and individuals. Nadine is a visionary, spiritual entrepreneur whose business and theater background provide the foundation for her roles as an inspiring author, dedicated educator, and dynamic leader in personal development. She was awarded Facilitator of the Year, 2010, by The Coaching Institute of Melbourne.

Nadine is passionate about contributing to the evolution of a resilient, sustainable, conscious global community. Her vision is to align with others who are inspiring and instructing people about how to live their boldest dreams and make their unique difference. She stands for the co-creation of a peaceful planet where nations take care of the Earth and of each other.

Nadine lives with her partner, Derek, and their daughter, Mira Moonbeam, in Queensland, Australia. Meet her and receive free personal development gifts at www.NadineLove.com.